AMERICAN WORLDVIEW INVENTORY 2021–2022

THE ANNUAL REPORT
ON THE STATE OF WORLDVIEW
IN THE UNITED STATES

GEORGE BARNA

American Worldview Inventory 2021–22
The Annual Report on the State of Worldview in the United States

Arizona Christian University Press is the book-publishing division of Arizona Christian University, a private Christian university in Glendale, Arizona, that provides a biblically integrated, liberal arts education equipping graduates to serve the Lord Jesus Christ in all aspects of life, as leaders of influence and excellence. Arizona Christian University exists to educate and equip followers of Christ to transform culture with truth.

Requests for permissions should be addressed to:

Arizona Christian University Press
1 W. Firestorm Way
Glendale, AZ 85306

ISBN: 978-1-7357763-4-7

Printed in the United States of America

TABLE OF CONTENTS

INTRODUCTION

Your worldview is a big deal. It defines who you are. It determines the choices you make. And yet, if you are like most Americans, you do not spend much time thinking about worldview. In fact, millions of people do not know that they have a worldview and are unable to identify what that term means.

Arizona Christian University initiated the Cultural Research Center, the institute responsible for the research and analysis contained in this book, to help rectify that situation. One of the primary thrusts of our efforts is to measure worldview and to expand and inform the national conversation about it. We developed a worldview measurement system—the Arizona Christian University Student Worldview Inventory—and use that instrument to conduct an annual census among our school's student body. We also conduct an annual, nationwide survey of a representative sample of American adults to track the worldview of people throughout the United States. And we have created a similar online tool—the ACU Worldview Assessment—that individuals, churches, and other organizations can use to identify and measure their worldview.

We are serious about worldview because it is a central component in determining the health and well-being of our nation and its people.

In the initial edition of the *American Worldview Inventory* series, we reported the findings from a major nationwide study we conducted in 2020 to determine how many Americans had a biblical worldview. That study substantially expanded the worldview research I have been conducting for several decades. We spent many months developing, testing, refining, and then re-testing a sophisticated data collection instrument before deploying that 68-question survey among a nationally representative sample of 2,000 adults. The results were eye-opening and provocative—and even somewhat controversial.

Because so much of this edition's research and analysis builds on the 2020 study, it may be helpful to review some of those foundational findings:

- A worldview is the filter through which you experience, interpret and respond to the world. It is, in essence, your decision-making filter.
- Everyone has a worldview. But not everyone has the same worldview.
- A person's worldview begins developing at the age of 15 to 18 months and is generally fully developed by the age of 13. During the teens and 20s, a person's worldview is tested, refined, reshaped, and articulated. After that stage the individual relies upon the resulting worldview without changing it much—unless there is a major life event or some type of supernatural intervention that instigates significant worldview transformation.
- Currently in the United States, an individual's worldview is developed largely by default, rather than intentionally and systematically.
- Major influences on worldview development include: messages from media, public policy, family and friends, and schools. Churches have less worldview influence than is widely assumed.
- Worldview is a combination of beliefs and behavior. You do what you believe. Therefore, you must think like Jesus if you want to live like Jesus.

- Once it has been formed, a person's worldview can be changed. But it is hard work, takes a lot of time and effort, and must be done strategically and intentionally to be effective. Most people do not experience significant worldview change during the course of their adult years.
- Only 6 percent of American adults possess a biblical worldview. The incidence was higher in certain portions of the population, such as theologically defined born-again Christians (19% had a biblical worldview), people who regularly attend an evangelical Christian church (21%), and SAGE Cons (44% among those who are Spiritually Active Governance Engaged Conservative Christians).
- We described people with a biblical worldview as Integrated Disciples because they have integrated their faith into every dimension of their life and live as *disciples* of Jesus Christ.
- An additional 19% of adults fit in the Emergent Follower category—individuals who do not qualify as having a biblical worldview, but whose worldview is greatly influenced by biblical truth and who could conceivably become Integrated Disciples given changes in their beliefs and behaviors.

Like the first volume of the *American Worldview Inventory Report (2020-21)*, this book is a modified compilation of a series of reports released during 2021 based upon the *American Worldview Inventory (AWVI)* conducted that year. This volume reports the findings of research that built on the earlier edition. Having discovered that just 6 percent of adults have a biblical worldview, we decided to address the natural follow-up question: What worldview(s) do the other 94 percent possess?

This year's version of the *AWVI* is the first large-scale, national exploration of the prevalence of competing worldviews in our country.

We tracked the incidence of seven major worldviews: Biblical Theism (i.e., the biblical worldview), Postmodernism, Secular Humanism, Moralistic Therapeutic Deism, Marxism, Eastern Mysticism, and Nihilism. In the pages that follow, you will discover what we learned—including information about the emergence of a "worldview" we did not anticipate: Syncretism.

The original news releases and other reports describing the research results have been edited and adapted for this volume. But the data have not changed. In some instances, additional data are included to clarify or amplify the analysis contained in the original documents.

I hope you find this book to be intellectually and spiritually interesting and challenging. If you would like to see our other recent worldview reports, visit our website at www.CulturalResearchCenter.com. The reports are accessible, free of charge, and can be shared with people you know. If you sign up on the website, we will send you alerts when new reports are available. On the website you will also learn about other worldview-related resources we offer.

George Barna
Glendale, Arizona
December 2021

CHAPTER 1

"SYNCRETISM" IS THE MOST COMMON WORLDVIEW AMONG U.S. ADULTS

Is there anything left in American society that's predictable?

Having researched trends in faith and culture for the past four decades, it seems that the only safe bet is that there is no safe bet! The choices that Americans have made during the past decade alone demonstrate how challenging it is to foresee the future.

- America has welcomed new forms of technology with open arms, radically changing the ways we live. The ubiquity of smart phones, social media, and the Internet has changed everything imaginable, including how we gather news and cultural information, how we conduct business, ways we make and maintain relationships, and the manner in which we arrange our schedules.
- Once a fiercely independent people, in recent years Americans have become more passive and compliant toward government authority. The nation's acquiescence to far-reaching government commands related to the Coronavirus pandemic is unprecedented.
- Identifying as a homosexual used to be done at great personal risk. But an estimated 2 percent of the population who lived as homosexual men or women successfully

spearheaded a major sexual orientation revolution. Today, a large majority of Americans believe that any sexual orientation is legitimate and deserves government protection. In fact, a study the Cultural Research Center conducted among Millennials, our youngest adult generation, revealed that three out of 10 members of that generation identify as LGBTQ.[1]

- Americans love their entertainment, but the substance of what they enjoy and how they receive it has changed drastically in just the last decade. Consider some of those shifts. We have gone from getting our music from CDs and radio, to streaming via services such as Apple Music, Pandora, and Spotify. We love movies but are less likely to journey to theaters or acquire DVDs to watch major-studio blockbusters. There has been a huge jump in viewership of movies created by independent studios and provided by streaming services. Broadcast and cable networks have lost market share to streaming services. Video products are increasing likely to be viewed on personal mobile devices rather than the family room television.
- Political activism was drastically declining until recently. Now, Millennials and political progressives have rejuvenated activism in the streets, turning the social media universe into a hotbed of activist rhetoric and calls to action.
- The national economy has been turned upside down by technological innovations. Amazon Prime is the new UPS. The gig economy has replaced traditional forms of employment. An enormous share of consumer activity now

takes place digitally. Millions of employees work from home, using tech tools to alleviate the need for centralized office space and in-person meetings.

- The "hot" social issues have transitioned to matters that were not even on the radar 20 years ago. Racial discrimination and reparations. Climate change initiatives, including the elimination of fossil fuels. The prosecution of "hate crimes." Support for extensive censorship of controversial ideas and perspectives. Sexual orientation rights and protection. The days of political campaigns succeeding based on a strategy of "It's the economy, stupid," are fading in the rearview mirror.

These are just a few examples of the radical and rapid transitions that have transformed the American way of life. But a shocking number of those changes have been facilitated by perhaps the most significant change of all—one that is virtually invisible to the public. I'm speaking about the revolution that has occurred in the prevailing worldview of Americans.

Everyone has a worldview—the filter we use to make sense of and respond to the world in ways that represent what we believe to be true, good, appropriate, and worthwhile. Before worldview research was introduced, most Americans called themselves Christian,[2] traditional biblical morality was widely accepted, church attendance was common, the Bible was revered as a special (and to many, holy) book, and we believed pastors when they told us that people had a biblical worldview.

Now that our worldview research is doing a deep dive into the philosophies of life that people actually embrace, and everything in our society seems to be changing, it is obvious that many of our past and current assumptions about who we are as Americans are wrong.

Maybe there was a time when most adults in this nation had a biblical worldview, but that is clearly not the situation now. We have the research to prove that. In fact, we would have to go a long way back—perhaps close to a century ago—to find a time when most Americans thought and acted biblically.

Thanks to research like the *American Worldview Inventory*, we know that very few Americans are currently Integrated Disciples (the term coined to describe people who possess a biblical worldview). Just six percent, to be precise—which is a lot fewer than most of us would have predicted.[3]

We have all seen the changes in national character over the last few decades and yet the 6% mark is still a shocking revelation and a troubling reality. As unsettling as the finding is, it begs an important question:

If only six percent of Americans have a biblical worldview, then what worldview do the other 94% hold?

It turns out the answer to this question is not a simple one. In fact, the research uncovers a result that is far from what we might have expected.

Three Mindboggling Outcomes

Here are three head-shaking outcomes from the 2021 worldview research conducted by the Cultural Research Center at Arizona Christian University:

First, the biblical worldview (known as Biblical Theism) remains the most widely held worldview in America. Even with a slim 6% incidence, it leads the pack. Yet with 94% of Americans essentially rejecting the biblical worldview as their preferred way to think and live, placing first is far from a resounding victory.

Second, the competing worldviews that constitute the gravest threats to biblical truth have failed to catch on as holistic philosophies of life. Those worldviews are:

- **Secular Humanism.** This worldview puts its faith in science and human reason, dismissing the existence of supernatural beings. It teaches that the universe erupted without any divine intervention and one of its products was humanity. This view contends that even though people have evolved over centuries of time, human beings are little more than biological machines. Secular humanists revere nature as the central, powerful force responsible for all that exists; therefore we must fiercely protect it. Morals and ethics are determined through application of science, reason, and experience. The goals of life are happiness and social justice. This view esteems fairness, tolerance, freedom, responsibility, and unity.
- **Postmodernism.** This philosophy of life rejects all large-scale narratives (such as Christianity or traditional anthropocentric history) used to explain our existence and progression. Instead, history, culture, and traditions are dismissed as artificial and contrived. Postmodernism rejects the imposition of truth principles, views material success as the goal of life, and generally "deconstructs" all forms of human organization and theory without offering alternatives. This philosophy of life was originally developed as a reaction to Marxism, which Postmodern thinkers vehemently rejected.
- **Eastern Mysticism.** An alternative to Western thought, this approach posits there is no personal God. Instead, this combination of Eastern philosophies contends that the prevailing force is the cosmos, of which we are all part, and through which we are all interrelated and interdependent. This view rejects God, absolute moral truths, and human reasoning. Instead, as part of the universal consciousness and continuity in which everything is part of the eternal,

impersonal life force, our life's goal is to transcend the material world to reach a unified spiritual expression. Buddhism and Hinduism are the best-known expressions of this philosophy, and a widely recognized adaptation of eastern principles is known as New Age.

- **Moralistic Therapeutic Deism.** A perversion of biblical Christianity, this philosophy believes that God exists but stays removed from humanity. He allows people to earn their salvation through their goodness and He has low standards for our earthly experience. MTD contends that our earthly purpose is to be happy, which comes from feeling good about self and being good to others. There are no absolute moral truths in this worldview. Instead, the Bible is a useful guidebook but not considered an infallible source of truth. This worldview is optimistic, driven by emotions, and human-centric.
- **Marxism.** Marxists say that life is best understood through the lens of oppression—particularly economic and political. Critical Race Theory, a derivative of Marxism, views race as potentially oppressive. The Marxist view, which serves as the philosophical underpinning of socialism and communism, dismisses organized religion, the Bible, the existence of God, life after death, the innate value of human life, and moral absolutes. It offers cultural elites as the hope of humankind due to their intellectual and moral superiority, and their willingness to lead the way forward. Marxism advocates abolishing family, marriage, individuality, tradition, and individual ownership of property.
- **Nihilism.** This philosophy of life rejects the supernatural, moral absolutes, ethical norms, and political and social institutions. Nihilism says that life has no meaning,

> purpose, truth, or value. Instead, life is pointless and random. This view claims that knowledge and meaning are illusions. Because nothing matters and there is no God to whom we answer, life is justifiably self-indulgent, but results in extreme pessimism and skepticism.

This new research shows that the worldviews that typically grab the most attention do not resonate with the American public. For example, Secular Humanism has been adopted by only 2% of the public. Just 1% of adults embrace Postmodernism or Nihilism. Although both Marxism (and Critical Theory) and Eastern Mysticism (or "New Age") receive a lot of media coverage, and elements of their perspectives and behaviors are common, less than one-half of one percent of American adults has adopted either of those worldviews. A sixth worldview that caused deep concern among evangelical Christians in the early 2000s—Moralistic Therapeutic Deism—has captured the hearts of 1% of American adults.

The Dominant Worldview Embraced by American Adults

Dominant Worldview	% of Adults
Biblical Worldview	6%
Secular Humanism	2%
Moralistic Therapeutic Deism	1%
Postmodernism	1%
Nihilism	1%
Eastern Mysticism	*
Marxism	*
Syncretism	88%

Note: *indicates less than one-half of one percent. Source: *American Worldview Inventory 2021*, Cultural Research Center at Arizona Christian University; N=2,000 U.S. Adults, 2021.

Keep in mind that these statistics represent the percentage of adults whose beliefs and behaviors reflect the principles and foundations of the worldview in question. These numbers do not reflect how many people describe themselves as having adopted or being adherents of the worldview in question.

Third, the big winner when it comes to worldview in America is "none of the above." Almost nine out of 10 U.S. adults (88%) have an impure, unrecognizable worldview that is nothing more than a customized, personal blend of disparate ideas adopted from multiple philosophies of life. This worldview is called Syncretism.

People who are driven by this unique, highly individualized mishmash of ideas simply combine them into what is usually an inconsistent, sometimes internally contradictory, hot mess of a worldview. Syncretism reflects the superficial thinking and feelings-based decision-making that prevails in our cut-and-paste society.

The Emergence of Syncretism

How did Syncretism become America's most prevalent worldview?

Since a worldview is a combination of beliefs and behaviors, it is possible for people to possess some of the beliefs or behaviors that reflect a particular worldview, but not enough to qualify as an adherent of that worldview.

But not embracing a specific, well-defined philosophy of life in its entirety does not mean that those worldviews lack influence.

The *AWVI 2021* data show that almost four out of 10 adults (39%) frequently turn to the principles of Moralistic Therapeutic Deism to shape their daily beliefs and behaviors—even though just 1% are full adherents of that perspective. It may well be, then, that this perspective—which amounts to a kind of fake Christianity, compromised by emotion, cultural preferences and spiritual inclusivism—has greater impact on America's thinking than any other worldview.

Meanwhile, the biblical worldview (Biblical Theism) emerged with 31% of adults regularly drawing from its tenets when they are making decisions. In other words, it is influential in their life to some degree, but far from a defining influence.

Almost one-sixth of Americans (16%) regularly rely upon Postmodern perspectives and behaviors even though only 1% possesses a comprehensive Postmodern worldview. The same proportion of adults (16%) regularly turns to Secular Humanist ideas in their decision-making, despite just 2% having adopted that worldview in full. One out of 10 adults (10%) has beliefs and behaviors that are regularly influenced by each of three other philosophies—Marxism, Eastern Mysticism and Nihilism—although very few Americans are full-fledged representatives of those worldviews.

Percentage of U.S. Adults Who Lean Either Strongly or Moderately Toward Specific Worldview Beliefs and Behaviors	
Worldview Beliefs and Behaviors	**% of Adults**
Moralistic Therapeutic Deism	39%
Biblical Worldview	31%
Secular Humanism	16%
Postmodernism	16%
Nihilism	10%
Eastern Mysticism	10%
Marxism	10%

Source: *American Worldview Inventory 2021*, Cultural Research Center at Arizona Christian University; N=2,000 U.S. Adults, 2021.

As is typically the case in research of this kind, certain subgroups of the population are more likely than others to lean toward specific worldviews, even if they do not fully represent those beliefs and behaviors. For instance:

- The biblical worldview is most attractive to SAGE Cons (Spiritually Active Governance Engaged Conservative Christians), theologically defined evangelicals (i.e., not self-described evangelicals), theologically defined born-again Christians (i.e., not necessarily those who call themselves "born again"), political conservatives, and registered Republicans.
- Moralistic Therapeutic Deism is most frequently relied upon by spiritual skeptics, people who consider themselves to be part of the LGBTQ community, people who are not registered to vote, political liberals, and individuals who attend a Catholic or predominantly black church.
- The people who are most likely to draw from the principles of Secular Humanism include spiritual skeptics, residents of the Western states, people 75 or older, and political liberals.
- U.S. adults most often attracted to Postmodern ideals are spiritual skeptics, residents of the Northeastern and Western states, people with a bachelor's degree, and political liberals.

Maybe at this point you're still puzzled by the dominance of Syncretism, wondering why more Americans have not adopted one of the well-defined, cohesive, comprehensive worldviews. One important reason is that Americans are not directly taught about worldview as they are raised. In that sense we can say that most people develop their worldview by default rather than by intent.

Think about how a person's worldview is established. My past research has shown that a worldview begins developing at 15-to-18 months of age and is almost fully formed by the age of 13. It is then tested and refined during one's teens and 20s before it is fully adopted and implemented. It rarely changes once people reach their 30s. During the developmental process, though, very few young people hear about or are intentionally taught about worldview.

And perhaps you would be disappointed or dismayed to discover how few Christian schools, religious congregations and Christian parents directly address worldview issues.

Instead, people generally adopt worldview beliefs and behaviors based on information derived from arts and entertainment, news reports, political statements or policies, and through conversations and experiences with people they trust.

In that sense, worldview is caught more than it is taught.

Institutions such as Arizona Christian University (ACU), where I teach and do research, are the exception to the rule. Every ACU class is intentionally and strategically taught through a biblical worldview lens. ACU is truly an aberration in American higher education. While there are several hundred Bible colleges and a few hundred more Christian colleges in the United States, surprisingly few of them are intentional and strategic about integrating biblical worldview development or reinforcement into every class and into their students' extracurricular experience. It takes years of holistic teaching, integration of thought and behavior, and support of biblically aligned choices before someone is likely to develop a biblical worldview.

Asleep at the Wheel

Unfortunately, American Christianity has been asleep at the worldview wheel for a long time—and the condition of the nation today reflects that failure. Some people dismiss the necessity of a systematic, prolonged worldview development process. They believe that knowing a few Bible verses, regularly attending church services that feature Bible-related sermons, plus some sincere praying will produce people who, like David, are seeking after God's own heart. Obviously, that approach to facilitating a worldview is not getting the job done.

Others argue that attending a Christian primary and secondary school will yield a biblical worldview. After all, they reason, Christian schools usually hire active Christians as teachers, feature chapel services, incorporate prayers during the school day, and require students to complete a religion class each year. While those are all fine components in the educational regimen, they alone do not result in students developing a biblical worldview.

A few well-intentioned parents have argued that expecting their children to follow the Ten Commandments is enough to develop a full-scale biblical worldview. It is not.

All those approaches represent token efforts, and are inadequate for developing an integrated body of beliefs and behaviors that enable someone to think like Jesus so they can then live like Jesus.

The recent uptick in concern about worldview as the foundation of people's decision-making process is a hopeful sign that Americans—and especially Bible-believing Christians—may be waking up to the importance of worldview development. While that revival of interest is encouraging, it is still an uphill battle to get Americans to take worldview development seriously.

Americans are neither deep nor sophisticated thinkers. We have largely abandoned logic and analytic thinking in favor of emotional satisfaction. To promote a way of life that challenges us to embrace biblical principles will take time and effort. Most people are more interested in a life of comfort and convenience than one of wisdom and righteousness. People who are willing to fight for a more biblical way of thinking and acting can make a difference, but they must be prepared to commit to the process for the long haul. A worldview is neither developed nor re-engineered overnight.

NOTES:

1. George Barna, *Millennials in America: New Insights into a Generation of Growing Influence*, October 2021, conducted by the Cultural Research Center at Arizona and commissioned by Foundations of Freedom. Available at: https://www.arizonachristian.edu/wp-content/uploads/2021/10/George-Barna-Millennial-Report-2021-FINAL-Web.pdf.
2. George Barna, Release #6: "What Does It Mean When People Say They Are 'Christian'?", *American Worldview Inventory 2021*, 31 August 2021, https://www.arizonachristian.edu/wp-content/uploads/2021/08/CRC_AWVI2021_Release06_Digital_01_20210831.pdf.
3. Unless otherwise noted, references to the current state of worldview in America are based on the annual, nationwide tracking study, *The American Worldview Inventory*, conducted by the Cultural Research Center at Arizona Christian University. More information about how the survey was conducted and other aspects of the research are provided in the Appendix of this book.

CHAPTER 2

COUNTERFEIT CHRISTIANITY: MORALISTIC THERAPEUTIC DEISM

In the previous chapter we established that Syncretism is the most common of all worldviews in America. And it isn't even a true worldview, but rather a collection of disparate worldview elements blended into a customized philosophy of life. But its prevalence raises a crucial question: Where do the ideas that comprise people's syncretistic views come from? The answer is those disparate views are taken from a variety of other, more cohesive philosophies, such as Postmodernism and Secular Humanism.

But the data from the *American Worldview Inventory 2021* is surprising—the worldview Americans are most likely to draw from is a relatively new and obscure philosophy of life known as Moralistic Therapeutic Deism—or MTD.

The Birth of a Worldview

This quietly popular but distorted form of Christianity was first identified infecting teenagers in the early 2000s. Some analysts predicted that as those young people matured, they would grow out of that worldview and embrace a more common, well-known worldview.

Unfortunately, that has not proven to be the case. The young people who originally made MTD "a thing" are now in their adult years. The research shows that millions in that generation still embrace the same tenets of Moralistic Therapeutic Deism that they adopted during their formative years. The persistence of MTD follows the well-established worldview developmental pattern: people form the worldview they will rely upon for the remainder of their life before they reach their teen years.

While this worldview doesn't get much respect—almost nobody has heard of it, including the people who have embraced it, and it is rarely included in discussions about worldview—it is a significant player in the worldview arena.

Moralistic Therapeutic Deism (MTD) was initially identified and named by sociologists Christian Smith and Melinda Lundquist Denton. In their 2005 book *Soul Searching: The Religious and Spiritual Lives of American Teenagers*,[1] they presented their findings from national research among teenagers at the turn of the millennium. Smith and Denton identified several core beliefs that characterized the thinking and behavior of American teens:

- Belief in a God who remains distant from people's lives.
- People are supposed to be good to each other (i.e., moral).
- The universal purpose of life is being happy and feeling good about oneself.
- There are no absolute moral truths.
- "Good people" earn their way into Heaven.
- God places very limited demands on people.

The Growth of MTD

What may have begun as a worldview primarily shared by teenagers and college students has enveloped a much larger segment of the population. Today, adults of all ages are more likely to lean on beliefs and behaviors drawn from MTD than from any of the other better-known worldviews examined. In total, nearly four out of 10 adults (39%) draw either heavily or moderately from the smorgasbord of beliefs represented by MTD, even though just 1% have MTD as their life-determining, dominant worldview.

Although three out of four people (74%) who lean substantially on MTD for life guidance consider themselves to be Christians, numerous beliefs held by this group conflict with biblical teaching. For instance:

- 95% do *not* consider success in life to be described as consistent obedience to God.
- 92% do *not* believe that the wealth they have has been given to them by God to manage for His purposes.
- 91% do *not* believe that people are born into sin and need to be saved by Jesus Christ.
- 88% say they get their primary moral guidance from various sources other than the Bible.
- 87% do *not* believe that the ultimate purpose of human life is to know, love, and serve God with all their heart, mind, strength, and soul.
- 76% contend that good people can earn a place in Heaven through their good behavior.
- 75% do *not* believe that God is the basis of all truth.
- 74% believe in karma.
- 73% say that having some type of religious faith is more important than which faith is embraced.
- 71% do *not* believe that the Bible is the true and reliable communication from God.

Other errant beliefs possessed by a majority of these adults include not holding an orthodox, biblical understanding of God; not believing in the Bible-based explanation of creation; rejecting the existence of absolute moral truth; denying the existence of the Holy Spirit; and believing it is possible to reach complete spiritual maturity within their lifetime.

Given these views it is not a shock to find that their behaviors and choices typically conflict with core biblical teachings. For instance, when it comes to moral considerations, a majority find the following behaviors to be either morally acceptable, or not a moral issue: having premarital sex with someone you expect to marry (a behavior supported by 83% of the MTD-influenced); breaking the speed limit (67%); having an abortion because raising the child would be stressful (59%); lying to protect one's personal reputation (58%); and claiming undeserved tax deductions that they are certain would not be detected by the government (51%).

Even though three-quarters of those substantially influenced by MTD claim to be Christian, only one-sixth (16%) qualify as born-again based on their theology (i.e., say they will go to Heaven only because they have confessed their sins and accepted Jesus Christ as their Savior).

As biblically vacuous as their religious beliefs may be, people drawn to Moralistic Therapeutic Deism are even less likely to engage in biblical faith practices. Just 13% of the people most influenced by MTD engage in faith practices that are robustly biblical. That percentage is less than half the proportion of similar religious activity found among all adults. The practices measured include reading the Bible, praying to God, confessing personal sins, pursuing God's will for their life and worshiping God.

MTD adherents are least likely to exhibit biblical ideals and actions when it comes to their lifestyle and personal relationships, or in their sense of purpose and calling. Americans generally have a weak commitment to the Bible, truth, and biblical morality. But adults who embrace MTD principles are substantially less committed than the typical American.

It is rare to find MTD proponents who consistently accept biblical principles related to truth, morality, lifestyle, and personal relationships. In fact, very few adults embrace biblical views and behaviors related to those areas. Less than 1% of adults in the MTD segment typically think or act in harmony with biblical principles on those matters.

Percentage of Moralistic Therapeutic Deism Adherents Who Possess Beliefs and Behaviors in a Category That Parallels Those of a Biblical Worldview			
	% of Adults Whose Beliefs and Behaviors in the Category Qualify as a Biblical Worldview		
Substantive Category of a Worldview	All Adults	MTD Adherents	Difference
Faith Practices	29%	13%	16 points
Lifestyle, Behaviors, Relationships	23	*	22
Family, Life, Values	20	4	16
Purpose and Calling	20	2	18
Sin, Salvation, God Relationship	15	2	13
God, Creation, History	15	8	7
Human Nature and Character	12	6	6
Bible, Truth, Morals	10	*	10

Note: "MTD Adherents" refers to people who have substantial reliance on MTD as a worldview. Source: *American Worldview Inventory 2021*, Cultural Research Center at Arizona Christian University, N=2,000 U.S. Adults, 2021.

Who Is Drawn to Moralistic Therapeutic Deism?

A large majority of those who are attracted to MTD consider themselves to be Christian. And almost half of those are Catholics, with the next largest chunk associated with churches that are traditionally black, Protestant congregations.

Among racial and ethnic segments, Hispanics showed the greatest alignment with MTD: a majority of them (52%) draw heavily or moderately from MTD perspectives. Realizing that a large share of the Hispanic population is Catholic—more than four out of 10—this outcome is not surprising.

There also was a significant age gap. People under age 50 were more than twice as likely as the 50-plus crowd to find MTD appealing. That is also expected given that the MTD phenomenon was first identified in research among teenagers who are now in their 30s or 40s.

Strikingly, about six out of 10 LGBTQ adults are consistently engaged with MTD. Although relatively few spiritual Skeptics embrace elements of MTD, individuals associated with Islam and Judaism were more likely than average to adopt many MTD tenets.

The Appeal of Moralistic Therapeutic Deism

Moralistic Therapeutic Deism is essentially a fake version of Christianity.

Young adults have grown up with a culturally adulterated version of the Christian faith, resulting in millions of them adopting a distorted version of genuine Christianity. The good news is practitioners of MTD are not anti-religion or anti-Christianity. They just are not willing to surrender to the demands of authentic Christianity—or to believe that a viable faith would even make such demands of them.

MTD is a generally optimistic, comforting form of religious faith, albeit one based on a twisted version of Christianity that emphasizes self rather than God, and relies on emotion rather than truth. For instance, those who adopt it believe in innate human goodness and kindness. They view God as a powerful but dispassionate observer who remains detached from human experience unless circumstances make Him the solution of last resort. They believe that life is about individual happiness and that action producing positive personal outcomes gives meaning and purpose to life. MTD is about believing in and promoting the best interests of self, reflected in currently popular cultural thinking. Its proponents may acknowledge the existence and some works of God, but they are not likely to prioritize knowing, loving and serving a transcendent God.

In the world of Moralistic Therapeutic Deists, the local church exists primarily to offer supportive and upbeat community, rather than worship, service, guidance toward holiness, or a genuine relationship with God. Because its foundations are abundantly pluralistic, those who champion this worldview encourage people to do whatever works, or whatever feels good, rather than that which fits with biblical principles. It is a worldview defined and driven by current culture more than by historic religious truths or a comprehensive and coherent doctrine. It asks little of its followers, while providing the comfort, convenience, and community those followers long for.

The Future

The prominence of MTD in American lives is a significant wake-up call to the biblical Church in our nation. The fact that a greater percentage of people who call themselves Christian draw from Moralistic Therapeutic Deism than rely on the Bible says a lot about the state of the Christian Church in America.

Simply and objectively stated, Christianity in America is rotting from the inside out.

Yet all is not lost. We can help the people attracted to MTD gain a better understanding of the basics of the Christian faith. Initial "fixes" would include helping them: develop a deeper understanding of the reliability and personal value of the Bible; embrace absolute moral truth; develop a true understanding of the love and human engagement of God; and recognize that our behavioral choices can reflect more authentic ways of "being good" and "doing right."

From a biblical perspective, all lost people have wandered off the path of righteousness, truth, and wisdom, no matter what alternative path they've chosen. That's a very human story. We can all claim to have lived that way for some period. After all, none of us was born into perfection, untainted by sin, and displaying perfect biblical theology and lifestyle choices. We all fall short of the glory and perfection of God, and need to be restored by His grace to His ways.

Just like those who live to know, love, and serve God through a biblical worldview with all their heart, mind, strength, and soul, those under the sway of Moralistic Therapeutic Deism can be led to the path of righteousness. Most of them are folks who want to do the right thing. They are not on a life trajectory that will enable it, but their journey can be realigned—if we are willing to understand their point of view and offer God's viable alternative.

NOTES:

1. Christian Smith and Melinda Lundquist Denton, *Soul Searching: The Religious and Spiritual Lives of American Teenagers* (Oxford: Oxford University Press, 2005).

CHAPTER 3

WHAT AMERICANS FIND ATTRACTIVE ABOUT MARXISM

An alarming number of U.S. adults—especially younger Americans—are embracing key tenets of the Marxist worldview, including negative views of private property, individual economic success, and traditional moral values.

America's increasing rejection of objective truth and loss of the biblical worldview has created a cultural context conducive to the growth of Marxist thought and practice. And in that context, many ideas reflecting the Marxist worldview may be unwittingly accepted by Americans who otherwise would reject the label "Marxist."

The *American Worldview Inventory 2021* reports that about one-quarter of U.S. adults holds negative views of private property. Specifically, 27% believe that allowing people to own property facilitates economic injustice, and almost as many (23%) believe that individual property ownership is bad for society. Such views are in direct conflict with biblical teaching. For instance, two of the Ten Commandments identify abuse of people's property as sin.[1] Several passages caution against changing the boundaries of the land that people own.[2] Other portions of scripture discuss people returning to the property they own.[3] Numbers 33:53-54 includes the command to take possession of specified land. Additional passages throughout the Bible address owning specific resources, such as animals.[4] There is little doubt that the Bible consistently supports ownership of the resources that God provides to individuals or allows them to possess. The role of government is to protect private property rights, not to outlaw, confiscate or redistribute personal possessions. Marxism, on the other hand, clearly calls for the abolition of private property.[5]

Millennials (ages 18 to 36 at the time of the survey) are far more likely than older adults to believe that private ownership of property is inappropriate or not part of the common good. Such views among the culture's emerging powerbrokers justify the concern that shifting worldviews among younger Americans will continue to fuel the growth of support for Marxism and its offshoots such as Critical Race Theory (or CRT) in American society.

Throughout the past decade national surveys have trumpeted the substantial proportion of U.S. adults who claim they would prefer socialism to capitalism, typically somewhere in the 30% to 40% range.

Millennials have displayed a particularly strong desire for a Marxist-based political system.

Overall, there are more than a dozen elements of the Marxist worldview that appeal to at least one-third of American adults. While less than 1% of American adults have adopted Marxism as their primary worldview, 10% consistently draw from the Marxist philosophy in their daily decision-making.

The research also shows that very few adults endorse two of the central tenets of Marxism—that marriage is harmful to society and that people are innately good but become corrupted by society.

Rarely a Dominant Worldview

Overall, less than 1% of Americans have adopted Marxism as their dominant worldview. If that proportion seems low, keep in mind that none of the seven well-defined worldviews we studied have a following that reaches double figures. The fact that Syncretism—the customized blend of elements drawn from a spectrum of competing worldviews—is the dominant worldview among Americans (88%) is indicative of the convoluted nature of people's intellectual, spiritual, and moral commitments.

But don't ignore the importance of another finding in the research—10% of adults consistently draw from the Marxist philosophy in their daily decision-making. That is much lower than the proportion of people who draw heavily from Moralistic Therapeutic Deism (39%) and Biblical Theism (i.e., the biblical worldview, at 31%), but it suggests that Marxism has a significant presence in our culture. In fact, it has the same breadth of influence on Americans' decision-making as do Nihilism and Eastern Mysticism, which are also consistently relied upon by about 10% of the public.

People, Property, and Wealth

While Marxism is not widely embraced as a comprehensive and defining philosophy of life, some of its principles are. For instance, two of the central tenets of the philosophy have been adopted by about one-quarter of adults. The notion that allowing people to own property facilitates economic injustice is accepted by 27%. Slightly fewer—23%—believe that individual property ownership is bad for society.

Some Marxist economic ideas have also developed a sizeable following. Almost one-fifth of adults (18%) believe that success is best described as living a healthy and productive life, unencumbered by economic oppression. A similar number (17%) believes that the personal accumulation of money and other forms of wealth are practices that demonstrate how unfair society can be to those who work hard yet are unable to get ahead.

Other Marxist ideals are wildly unpopular. For example, only one in 20 adults (5%) claims that the primary source of guidance for personal moral decisions should be government laws or direction provided by political leaders. A mere 6% agree with Karl Marx's dictum that marriage is harmful to society and is a practice that should be eliminated. And barely one out of every 10 adults (11%) accepts the Marxist idea that people were originally good but became corrupted by society.

Millions of Americans Embrace Marxist Views about Race, Money & Success (Percentage of U.S. adults who embrace the outlook described)	
Race is used by white people to advance their economic and political interests at the expense of people of color	41%
Allowing people to own property facilitates economic injustice	27%
Success is living a healthy and productive life, without economic oppression	18%
The personal accumulation of money and other forms of wealth is an example of how unfair society can be to those who work hard but do not get ahead	17%
Source: *American Worldview Inventory 2021*, Cultural Research Center at Arizona Christian University; N=2,000 U.S Adults, 2021.	

Marx and his devotees recognized that belief in a powerful supernatural deity who controls all things was a dire threat to his vision for humankind. He worked hard to disabuse people of the notion that God exists. It's no wonder that Marx viewed God and the Bible as such threats. After all, the biblical worldview—starting with the Ten Commandments—commands people to not steal or covet the private property of others; teaches that greed and envy are sinful; and that work that produces wealth to pay for food and shelter is an important and necessary part of life and human flourishing. It goes on to encourage those who are blessed with any degree of wealth to voluntarily give a portion of that wealth to help the poor. It also instructs the poor they are not entitled to steal private property from the rich and they should not envy their wealth.

Marxism and Faith

Marxist ideology denies the existence of God or a living deity in favor of vesting authority in government and social elites. Although a slight majority of adults in the United States (52%) still believes in the existence of some type of transcendent, supernatural being(s), the most rapidly growing religious segment of the population (34%) contends that they don't believe, know, or care whether God exists. This expanding niche—labeled the Don'ts—represents a spiritual foundation that is compatible with Marxist thought and practice and could facilitate the expansion of the ideology.

The Prevalence of Marxist Views on Creation & Humanity (Percentage of U.S. adults who embrace the outlook described)	
Human beings have developed over a long time from less advanced forms of life in a process that occurred naturally, without any supernatural intervention	48%
There is no such thing as God; or a higher power may exist, but nobody really knows for certain; or don't know what to believe about the existence of God or a higher power	34%
The universe came into existence without any type of divine assistance; it is solely a physical phenomenon	34%
History is a human narrative, so it may differ from person to person	24%
Man is a biological machine whose natural goodness is inevitably corrupted by society	23%
Source: *American Worldview Inventory 2021*, Cultural Research Center at Arizona Christian University; N=2,000 U.S. Adults, 2021.	

There are a variety of other religious and philosophical beliefs that tens of millions of Americans embrace that are compatible with Marxism. For instance, six out of 10 adults reject the existence of absolute or objective moral truth. A plurality of adults believes in evolution. And the increasingly widespread doubts about the reliability of the Bible facilitate alternative sources of moral guidance and lifestyle boundaries.

These shifts in religious and philosophical beliefs away from God and biblical truth create a climate conducive to broader acceptance of Marxist ideas.

Truth and Morality, Marxist Style (Percentage of U.S. adults who embrace the outlook described)	
Determining moral truth is up to each individual; there are no moral absolutes that apply to everyone, all the time	54%
Objective moral truth does not exist; all moral truth is personal and subjective	42%
Having sexual relations with someone you love and expect to marry in the future is morally acceptable	68%
Having an abortion because one's partner has left, and the mother knows she cannot reasonably take care of the child, is morally acceptable	48%
Telling a falsehood of minor consequence in order to protect personal interests or reputation is morally acceptable	43%
Regardless of the motivation, suicide and euthanasia are morally acceptable choices	32%
Source: *American Worldview Inventory 2021*, Cultural Research Center at Arizona Christian University; N=2,000 U.S. Adults, 2021.	

Marxism and Moral Choices

Over the past two decades Americans have been abandoning biblical morality. And increasingly, many common moral choices in the United States these days are consistent with Marxist ideals.

Two-thirds of adults (68%) say that sexual relations outside of marriage are morally tenable. Given the Marxist dogma that marriage is a form of sexual and economic oppression, unfettered sexual expression fits the Marxist framework.[6]

Half of U.S. adults (48%) believe that having an abortion because their partner left, making care of the child difficult, is also morally reasonable. Because Marxism does not value human life, and prioritizing children over the state is counterproductive to the Marxist vision, abortion is viewed as a legitimate, useful option. To a Marxist, abortion is not a moral issue.

And more than four of every 10 people (43%) believe that lying to protect one's best interests or reputation is morally acceptable. Marxism, of course, does not support the idea of absolute or objective moral truth, so personal deceptions are accepted as a way of life in which the ends justify the means.

Without a firm belief in the existence of an active, personal God who has provided moral guidance to us through the Bible and to whom we are accountable, behaviors that were once thought to be immoral are now considered by large numbers of Americans to be defensible matters of personal choice. That perspective enables people to increasingly embrace points of view that are consistent with Marxist ideals and lifestyles.

Critical Race Theory

One of the more controversial worldviews these days is an offshoot of Marxism known as Critical Theory. It is an eclectic, multi-disciplinary approach to explaining and addressing forms of oppression based on personal identity, especially racial identity.

Critical Race Theory (popularly known as CRT) is part of the larger Critical Theory philosophy that seeks social transformation based on ending racial oppression through a multi-faceted reliance upon race-based narratives, black nationalism, calling out the alleged existence of institutionalized racism, and bringing attention to "interest convergence" (i.e., racism that advances the personal interests of the oppressor). CRT also advocates "intersectionality"—that is, race intersects with class, gender and sexual orientation to inform a person's identity and thereby produces complex forms of oppression.

In effect, CRT is a kind of "Trojan Horse" for the advancement of Marxism. Its supporters often position Critical Race Theory as a means of extinguishing hurtful and unjust acts of racism by promoting racial sensitivity and rectifying inaccurate historical interpretations.

But Christopher Rufo, a Senior Fellow at the Manhattan Institute, notes that CRT contends that "America is an irredeemably racist nation" and its constitutional principles of freedom and equality "are mere 'camouflages'... for white supremacy."[7] He further explains that CRT "seeks to use race as a means of moral, social and political revolution" and cites prominent advocates of CRT who seek to use the social theory as a means of abolishing capitalism and installing a "near omnipotent federal bureaucracy with the power to nullify and law or silence political speech that isn't antiracist."[8]

A large, deep-pocketed and influential assemblage of corporations and social advocacy entities has thrown its weight behind the nascent CRT movement. Hundreds of major corporations, ranging from those who are immersed in "woke" or "cancel" culture (e.g., Apple, Microsoft, Amazon, Twitter and many others) are backing this neo-Marxist offshoot. But so are some organizations whose involvement may come as a surprise to the average consumer. Companies such as Walmart, Sony, IBM, Coca-Cola and Verizon have initiated employee training programs based on CRT principles and perspectives, or have funded pro-CRT activities.

The political and social activist realms have jumped into the fray, as well. The U.S. Conference of Mayors adopted a resolution supporting the promotion of CRT in public school classrooms.[9] President Biden signed an Executive Order to advance CRT in the federal workplace.[10]Advocacy groups including the 1619 Project (originating at *The New York Times*), the National Education Association (NEA), the nation's largest teachers' union, Black Lives Matter and American Association of University Professors have been aggressively pushing CRT. The economic muscle of pro-CRT organizations has enabled the Marxist-based philosophy to garner heavy media coverage and integration into the national conversation about who we are and how we should live.

The research we conducted did not delve specifically into Critical Race Theory beyond its Marxist roots. However, our survey did reveal that 41% of U.S. adults believe that race is used by white people to advance their own economic and political interests at the expense of people of color. This belief reflects the CRT philosophy.

Like Marxism, Critical Race Theory is generally opposed to biblical ideas. The biblical worldview holds that all people are created equal by God, and that each person—no matter their race, gender or level of wealth—should be treated equally and with respect as a person created in the image of God. The biblical worldview rejects racism, racial categorization, identity and race-based politics, and breaks down barriers while promoting unity through a relationship with Jesus Christ that makes all men and women brothers and sisters, part of the family of God, and worthy of human dignity, respect, and love.

Millennials Are More Accepting of Marxism

Much of the newfound energy behind Marxism comes from young adults. Millennials have consistently emerged as the generation most supportive of socialism, the entry-level political application of Marxist ideology. The youngest adult generation, aged 18 through 36 at the time of the survey, is leading the way toward adopting ideas that facilitate socialist and Marxist activity.

Millennials were notably *more* likely than their elders to possess a variety of beliefs that are consistent with Marxist thought and action:

- Determining moral truth is up to each individual; there are no moral absolutes that apply to everyone, all the time.

- Objective moral truth does not exist; all moral truth is personal and subjective.
- Don't know, don't care, or don't believe in the existence of a supernatural, personal, living God.
- People are merely biological machines whose natural goodness is inevitably corrupted by society.
- The personal accumulation of money and other forms of wealth exemplify how unfair society can be toward those who work hard but do not get ahead.
- Allowing people to own property facilitates economic injustice.
- Individual property ownership is bad for society.
- Race is used by white people to advance their economic and political interests at the expense of people of color.
- Lying to protect personal interests or reputation is morally acceptable.
- Having an abortion because one's partner left, making it difficult or a hardship to care for the child, is morally acceptable.
- Having sexual relations with someone you love and expect to marry in the future is morally acceptable.
- Regardless of the motivation, suicide and euthanasia are morally acceptable choices.
- More likely to consider themselves to be LGBTQ.

In addition to Millennials, non-white individuals were more likely than whites to accept some of the ideas that fit with Marxism. Among those were the rejection of God and absolute moral truth; agreeing that property ownership fosters economic injustice; the belief that whites use race for their own benefit at the expense of non-whites; believing human life is not sacred; and moral behaviors are better decided based on personal best interest than any kind of standard, unchanging principles or truths.

Conditions are Ripe for Expansion of Marxism

Although America has few citizens whose life philosophy is undeniably Marxist, the table is set for Marxism to grow in this nation.

Previous surveys examining attitudes related to socialism and Marxism show that most Americans do not understand the foundations of socialism, or that socialism and Marxism are joined at the hip.[11] The increasing rejection of basic biblical principles by adults has left an ideological vacuum that Marxism and its offshoots, such as Critical Race Theory, are seeking to fill.

A Marxist revolution within the United States is not as far-fetched as some people assume. Consider the experience of the LGBTQ community. Its well-conceived and meticulously executed long-term plan for growth smoothed the way for radical changes in the law and in the way Americans think about gender identity and sexual orientation. They accomplished their goals despite being less than 3% of the population. Movements that are small in the number of passionate supporters but are well-funded, highly disciplined, and adroitly execute strategic plans can transform the larger culture despite their tiny size.

As we consider the potential of non-biblical worldviews such as Marxism to introduce radical changes or even replace our existing institutions and social system, we cannot afford to be dismissive. Most Americans do not realize they already support elements of Marxist ideology. A large share of the youngest adult generation—the Millennials—has positive feelings about socialism. Those realities combine with powerful and strategically placed government officials and agencies currently putting Marxist ideals into practice.

Only a fool would conclude that it is not feasible that America could unwittingly embrace an increasing number of Marxist principles and practices during the coming years, leading to a socialist or Marxist takeover. Such a grand makeover is neither imminent nor inevitable—but, as the worldview data point out, neither is it beyond the realm of possibility.

NOTES:

1. Exodus 20:15, 20:17.
2. Deuteronomy 19:14, 27:17; Proverbs 23:10,22:28.
3. Leviticus 25:10.
4. Exodus 21:29.
5. The abolition of private property is the guiding principle of Marxism, as advocated in Karl Marx's revolutionary program found in *The Communist Manifesto*, first published in 1848. See: Karl Marx and Friedrich Engels, The Communist Manifesto (Chicago: Charles H. Kerr, 1888). Available at: https://www.gutenberg.org/files/61/61-h/61-h.htm
6. This view closely parallels Marx's view of marriage found in The Communist Manifesto. In it, Marx calls for the abolition of marriage on the grounds that women are used as property and also equates marriage to private prostitution.
7. Christopher Rufo, "Battle Over Critical Race Theory," *Wall Street Journal* Opinion, June 27, 2021.
8. Ibid.
9. "In Support of Critical Race Theory in Public K-12 Education (Resolution 68)," U.S. Conference of Mayors, 89th Annual Meeting, August 31 to September 4, 2021. https://legacy.usmayors.org/resolutions/89th_Conference/proposed-review-list-full-print-committee-individual.asp?resid=a0F4N00000PTL6pUAH
10. "Fact Sheet: President Biden Signs Executive Order Advancing Diversity, Equity, Inclusion, and Accessibility in the Federal Government," June 25, 2021. https://www.whitehouse.gov/briefing-room/statements-releases/2021/06/25/fact-sheet-president-biden-signs-executive-order-advancing-diversityi-equity-inclusion-and-accessibility-in-the-federal-government
11. George Barna, "Americans Favor Capitalism, Tempted by Socialism, Ill-Informed about Both," American Culture Review, March 28, 2018.

CHAPTER 4

THE INFLUENCE OF POSTMODERNISM AND SECULAR HUMANISM

Our culture is full of worldviews that run counter to the biblical worldview. Two that have been widely discussed for several decades are Postmodernism and Secular Humanism. While neither of them is thoroughly embraced by a large share of Americans, elements of both philosophies are routinely accepted and acted upon—without most people realizing that they are appropriating those points of view.

As noted earlier, nine out of 10 adults (88%) have a worldview best described as Syncretism, a unique worldview fashioned from the personally appealing parts of other worldviews. Of the seven competing worldviews measured by the *American Worldview Inventory 2021*, Postmodernism and Secular Humanism contribute significantly to the customized worldviews of Americans.

Overall, only 2% of adults have adopted Secular Humanism as their dominant worldview, consistently thinking and acting in ways that are in harmony with the foundational tenets of that philosophy of life. Yet one out of every six adults (16%) regularly thinks or acts in ways that reflect the principles of Secular Humanism.

Similarly, Postmodernism has been embraced as the dominant worldview by only 1% of the public, but it frequently forms the basis of the choices of 16% of U.S. adults.

Those statistics suggest that Secular Humanism and Postmodernism are widely utilized worldviews, trailing only Biblical Theism (i.e., the biblical worldview) and Moralistic Therapeutic Deism, as the life philosophies that Americans most often rely on to guide their decision-making.

Most Americans do not know what worldviews they possess or draw from in their daily decision-making. A large share of American adults would be surprised to discover that many of their beliefs and behaviors are consistent with worldviews such as Postmodernism, Secular Humanism, Marxism, and Eastern Mysticism.

Postmodernism in America

The worldview known as Postmodernism is an extension of another worldview, Existentialism. The Postmodern worldview is based on ideas such as belief that all knowledge, values, and morals are dependent on and largely determined by social conditions. There is no absolute moral truth or universal moral boundaries. Science and reason are of limited value to personal and societal progress. And everything, including personal identity and social roles, is constantly changing.

Befitting a worldview that dismisses the importance, if not the very existence, of God, Postmodernism is very self-focused. It is skeptical or dismissive of large-scale narratives (or metanarratives) that seek to explain our existence and experience, especially religious narratives such as Christianity.

Postmodern thought is at the forefront of the emerging, non-traditional moral order in America. The foundation of such thought is that all truth is subjective and that there are no moral absolutes—a perspective held by 54% of Americans.

Those who embrace Postmodernism are more accepting than other people of breaches of traditional morality. For instance, lies or deceptions that protect an individual or are based upon an alternative view of the causal circumstances are deemed viable in a Postmodern world. Similarly, incidents of theft or cheating that aid someone in need could be justified. Sexual relations outside of marriage is a behavior that would not trouble those embracing Postmodern views.

Although most Americans describe themselves as Christian, four out of every 10 adults (41%) reject the notion that every moral choice we make either honors or dishonors God. That is consistent with Postmodern thinking, which claims both that there may not be a supernatural being to whom we answer and that our moral choices are about our life rather than fulfilling the expectations or rules of a supernatural being.

Given its doubts about the existence of God, and believing that there are no all-inclusive religious principles, commands, truths, or teachings that should direct our choices, it is natural to find that Postmodernism advocates are offended by Christian evangelism. What may be more surprising, though, is the fact that more than one-third of all U.S. adults share that view, deeming proselytizing to be untenable.

Other common Postmodern ideas that are widely accepted by adults in the United States include:

- 39% claim that human life has no intrinsic value.
- 29% express their commitment to getting even with those who wrong them.
- 29% believe there is no way of knowing whether God or a supernatural being exists.
- 28% indicate that they treat people based on their current feelings and circumstances.

- 24% believe that historical narratives are unreliable because they are subjective human perspectives.

Secular Humanism in America

Postmodernism is one of the most influential worldviews chipping away at the standing of Biblical Theism. But it is not alone in separating Americans from biblical wisdom and living. The worldview research demonstrates that Secular Humanism, the targeted "boogeyman" of the Church during the 1980s, remains a force to be reckoned with.

Over the years, Secular Humanists (who sometimes prefer to be called simply "humanists" or whose worldview is sometimes referred to as Naturalism) have composed numerous declarations to define their philosophy. Secular Humanism includes a number of elements, such as: the centrality of human reason and scientific inquiry to point the way forward; a desire to develop a more humane and moral society through human effort and capabilities; disbelief in a supernatural deity, an afterlife, absolute moral truth, and any philosophy based on religious faith; and a pursuit of fairness, justice, and tolerance.

Millions of Americans have bought into the Secular Humanist way of thinking and living, whether knowingly or naively. Some of the more common expressions of Secular Humanism held by millions of people include:

- 54% believe the universe had a scientifically explainable beginning; it was not created through any type of supernatural intervention.
- 48% contend that human beings are the result of an explicable evolutionary process; the worldview rejects the idea that humans were created by God or are made in His likeness.

- 36% identify "success" in life as the various human accomplishments that produce happiness or a sense of fulfillment.
- 33% say that their primary guide to morality is human reason.
- 24% believe that truth can only be determined through scientific inquiry and proof.

Other Secular Humanist beliefs are less widely accepted by Americans such as atheism—only 6% believe there is no such thing as God, a supreme being, or a supernatural being.

Biblical Worldview Distinctives

The research brings to light the beliefs and behaviors of the biblical worldview—most of which are rejected by Postmodernism and Secular Humanism.

While Postmodernism cautions people against sharing their personal faith views, the biblical worldview encourages people to do so as an act of love, making the grace of God real and accessible for those who need His forgiveness and acceptance.

While Secular Humanism promotes material progress as the foundation of meaning and success, the biblical worldview sees single-minded materialistic pursuits as a distraction, if not outright idolatry.

Postmodernism does not teach that human life has great value. The biblical worldview does, pointing out that humans were created by God, made in His image and for His purposes, are worthy of respect because of that heritage, and that God describes life as a gift.

Although both Postmodernism and Secular Humanism hold that absolute moral truth does not exist, the biblical worldview champions its existence, pointing to the proven and indisputable truth principles

A Comparison of the Beliefs of People Who Rely Upon Biblical Theism, Secular Humanism, or Postmodernism				
			Draws heavily from:	
Belief	All U.S. Adults	Have a BWV	Secular Humanism	Post-modernism
Our understanding of reality is based on cultural interpretation	22%	*	33%	65%
Human beings are just biological machines corrupted by society	23	*	69	62
Success is best described as consistent obedience to God	21	98	1	*
The basis of truth is scientific proof	24	*	75	44
The basis of truth is God, as revealed in the Bible	41	99	4	*
Human beings developed over a long period of time, from less advanced forms of life, without supernatural intervention	48	2	87	78
Don't know, believe, or care if God exists	34	0	85	87
There is no life after death on earth	16	0	69	53

Source: *American Worldview Inventory 2021*, Cultural Research Center at Arizona Christian University; N=2,000 U.S. Adults, 2021. Due to space limitations, belief descriptions are not the exact wording used in the survey. Abbreviations: BWV = Biblical Worldview; * indicates less than one-half of one percent.

in the Bible as authored by God, provided in a form we can access and understand, and relevant to our ability to discern the meaning of life and our role in the unfolding of God's larger narrative for humanity. It is those truth principles that ought to shape our moral choices, rather than accepting the self-indulgent and acquiescent morality standards of Secular Humanism and Postmodernism.

CHAPTER 5

TEN SEDUCTIVE UNBIBLICAL IDEAS WIDELY EMBRACED BY AMERICANS

The American public flaunts its free will in many ways, not the least of which is by embracing some seductive—but decidedly unbiblical—beliefs as part of their worldview.

In fact, worldview research leads to a list of 10 prevalent "seductive unbiblical ideas" embraced by American adults. From a biblical point of view, the items on this list are almost as foolish as what we used to get on comedian and TV host David Letterman's nightly Top 10 lists. But this is no joke: Americans really believe this stuff. Here are leading candidates for the Top 10 biblically indefensible beliefs:

- Having faith matters more than what faith you have.
- All faiths are of equal value.
- Belief in "karma," the idea rooted in Eastern religions that "you get what you give."
- There is no absolute moral truth.
- All moral truth is personal and subjective.
- People are "basically good."
- Success is determined by happiness, comfort, goodness, or fulfilled potential.
- Sexual relations apart from marriage are morally acceptable.

- People are not inherently sinful.
- The accumulation of personal wealth is unrelated to God's blessings or purposes.

Amazingly, even the 6% of adults who have a biblical worldview harbor many of these counter-biblical ideas as part of their personal philosophy of life.

Based on more than five dozen worldview-related questions we posed to adults, the most egregious departures from biblical teaching relate to faith selection, personal behavior, individual decision-making, the human condition, and life outcomes.

Faith Selection

Most adults in the United States (62%) believe that "having faith matters more than which faith you have." That perspective coincides with another counter-biblical view held by a large majority (62%): "all religious faiths are of equal value."

Those views were most common among people attending Catholic or mainline Protestant churches, as well as those who are affiliated with non-Christian religions. Other segments who embraced these views comparatively often were Democrats, liberals, and people living in wealthier households.

Such inclusive religious thinking is a product of worldviews such as Postmodernism, which teaches that there is no way to know whether God exists, but having a faith that serves your needs and purposes is a valid personal choice.

Surprisingly, nearly half of all individuals who have a biblical worldview (42%) accept the idea that having some type of faith matters more than which one. Put differently, even though a large majority of adults with a biblical worldview embraces Christianity as their faith of choice and have accepted Jesus Christ as their personal Lord and Savior, close to half of them do not support Christianity's claim to exclusivity.

Yet, the Bible clearly teaches that the Judeo-Christian faith is the only valid spiritual pathway. Some criticize Christianity for being an exclusive faith—the "one true faith"—as arrogant and elitist. But the Bible notes that people are called by their Creator God to love, worship and serve only Him and that all other deities are merely idols (Ps. 96:4,5; Phil. 2:9-11; Deut. 6:13-14). Jesus Christ is revealed as the living God with whom a grace-based relationship is the only way to eternal peace with God (John 14:6, Acts 4:12).

Personal Behavior

Although Eastern Mysticism is not knowingly embraced by many Americans—less than 1% follow it as their dominant worldview—some of its beliefs have nestled their way into the hearts and minds of many people. Karma is one of those beliefs. Nearly six out of 10 adults (57%) say they believe in karma. In fact, the concept has become so comfortable to Americans that one-third of the people with the biblical worldview (33%) also embrace this concept.

Many people contend that karma is a valid and spiritually harmless principle. It refers to cause and effect; what you have done in the past or present will produce predictable outcomes in your future. It is related to the idea of reincarnation—what you do in this life will determine the nature of your next life, after your "rebirth." In total, 9% of American adults expect to be reincarnated, and four out of 10 (39%) believe such a "rebirth" is "a real possibility" for them. That concept conflicts with biblical teaching that we die once (Heb. 9:27) and God determines our fate. As such, Christians view life as a God-directed journey, not a self-determined cycle.

Similarly, despite the cultural cache it has, karma is not a biblical perspective. Some argue that the idea resembles Paul's exhortation that a person will reap what he or she sows (Gal. 6:7). However, that passage relates to what will happen to a person when they face God's judgment. Rather than personally determining our future through our actions, it is God who directs the footsteps of human beings and determines their destiny.

While karma is considered by its defenders to be inescapable—you get what you deserve—the Bible suggests that because God will forgive those who earnestly seek His grace, our physical actions do not automatically result in inevitable spiritual outcomes. In fact, one of the great benefits of being a disciple of Jesus is that because of His redeeming death and resurrection, those who confess their sins and claim Him as their savior do not get what they deserve!

Karma teaches that an impersonal force is behind our future, and reality shows that people sometimes get what they deserve—but sometimes they do not. In contrast, the Bible teaches that a personal, engaged Creator uniquely and predictably rewards and punishes every individual based upon His explicit life principles, leaving nothing to chance—but that His response is not always immediate, obvious, or happens in this world. In a world driven by karma, human beings determine their own future; in God's universe, everyone's present and future is in His hands.

But karma is not the only unorthodox idea that most Americans have adopted. Two-thirds of adults (68%) now contend that premarital sex between two people who believe they love each other is either morally acceptable or not even a moral issue. This thinking is endorsed by people heavily influenced by various worldviews, such as Secular Humanism, Moralistic Therapeutic Deism, and Marxism. To their credit, a mere 2% of adults who possess the biblical worldview concur that premarital sex is morally acceptable.

While American culture has become increasingly casual about sexual relations, the Bible is clear that such relations are to occur only within the context of marriage. (1 Cor. 6:18-20, 1 Cor. 7:1-2, 1 Cor. 7:8-9). Sexual relations among people who are married, but not to each other (commonly known as adultery) are also forbidden.

Acceptance of premarital sex is especially widespread among spiritual skeptics (88%), residents of the Northeast (79%), and self-identified LGBTQ adults (78%). An overwhelming majority of people who draw their worldview heavily from any of the non-biblical worldviews endorse premarital sex, ranging from 81% of those who frequently rely on Nihilist philosophy to 96% of those who draw heavily from Postmodern perspectives.

Unfortunately, nearly half of all theologically identified born-again individuals (43%) accept premarital sex as morally acceptable.

Decision-making

The declining influence of the Bible in American culture—and along with it, the belief that absolute moral truth exists—is evident in how people make decisions that determine their behaviors.

Do Americans seek to know and understand moral absolutes? No, because most of them no longer believe that such unconditional parameters exist. Overall, two out of three adults (67%) argue that there are no moral absolutes. Six out of 10 (58%) contend that moral truth is determined by each person based upon what seems right to them. Consistent with that view, only four out of 10 (39%) say that objective moral truth exists.

Most people (70%) rely upon their feelings, experiences, or the counsel of family and friends to decide what is right and wrong. Relatively few (31%) identify the Bible as their primary source of moral guidance. This situation is reminiscent of the scriptural passage describing how people abandoned God's truth and did whatever seemed right in their own eyes (Judges 17:6).

The rejection of absolute, objective moral truth is a predictable consequence for a nation in which only 6% of adults have a biblical worldview. All the other major worldviews that are demonstrably influencing Americans argue that truth is subjective, conditional, and personal.

Indisputably, millions of Americans have moved away from believing that the Bible contains relevant and reliable moral absolutes for their life. Yet the Bible explains that it is God's guidance, designed to affect every dimension of our life with His truth (2 Tim. 3:16). To prepare His people to live successful lives, God provided us with everything required to live a godly life, including the Bible (2 Pet. 1: 3-7, 19-21). We are assured that His Law is right and true and serves our best interests when it is followed (John 17:17, Romans 7:12).

The Human Condition

Without the Bible as a guidebook for life, it is not surprising that people are confused about how life works. For instance, three out of four adults reject the idea that humans are born into sin and need to be saved from the consequences of that spiritual defect by Jesus Christ. Only 25% believe in the concept of original sin and redemption through Jesus. Complementing that view, seven out of 10 Americans (69%) maintain that people are basically good.

Worldviews that conflict with the biblical perspective deny or downplay sin. For instance, Marxism teaches that people were originally good but were corrupted by society. Secular Humanism posits that people are neither good nor bad, they are who they are. The view of Eastern

Mysticism is that everyone is a divine creature engaged in the eternal pursuit of a perfected consciousness and cosmic unity, but certainly not inherently sinful.

The biblical narrative tells a different story. It famously describes how Adam and Eve sinned and passed along a heritage of sinfulness to all of humanity (Rom. 5:12, 18; Ps. 51:5). The result is that no one is protected from having a sinful nature (Ps. 14:2-3, Luke 18:19). We cannot overcome the effects of sin without appropriating the grace of God through the death and resurrection of Jesus Christ for our personal spiritual, eternal redemption.

Yet most Americans believe in their own goodness and are not overly concerned about the effects of sin, even if they believe sin may exist. The people especially impervious to the flawed nature of humanity are those associated with non-Christian faiths or with no faith system. The goodness of human beings is widely accepted by Millennials, political liberals, upscale individuals, and residents of the Northeast.

A group you might expect to reject the view that "people are inherently good" are those categorized as born-again Christians because of their theological beliefs about sin and salvation. Yet the most recent *American Worldview Inventory* found that a shockingly large percentage of theologically defined born-again Christians (44%) does not accept the idea that people are born into sin. And a large majority of them (69%) also embraces the notion that all people are basically good.

Life Outcomes

When it comes to life outcomes, the views of people who have a biblical worldview and those who do not are dramatically different.

For instance, four out of five people with a biblical worldview believe that the personal accumulation of wealth has been entrusted to them by God to manage for His purposes (81%). However, just one out of five other adults (19%) embraces that belief. Common alternative views about wealth are: it is earned and deserved; it reflects how unfair society can be toward those who work hard but do not get ahead; or that it is supplied for personal survival and pleasure.

Overall, the people least likely to accept wealth as a matter of stewardship for God's purposes included non-Christians and Skeptics, Millennials, Hispanics, and liberals. Only a minority of theologically defined born-again Christians (42%) embraced the notion of wealth as a gift from God to invest for His kingdom.

Adults with a biblical worldview almost universally agreed that success is best indicated by consistent obedience to God (98%). But nationwide just one out of five people (21%) adopts that perspective. In their minds, success was more likely to be defined as being a "good person" (a chief ideal of Moralistic Therapeutic Deism), experiencing happiness or freedom (a view pushed by Postmodernism), or living a healthy and productive life without economic oppression (a Marxist objective).

Points in Common

If you reflect on these belief patterns you will see that these seductive unbiblical perspectives have two factors in common: control and pleasure.

Consider how these counter-biblical concepts provide their acolytes with control. In some cases, it's about taking charge of our destiny or spirituality. In other cases, it's about determining the definitions and boundaries related to truth, morality, or resource management. It seems that most Americans are searching for ways to exert control over every aspect of their lives.

Biblical Christianity often poses unnatural, unexpected life principles. The scriptures do not encourage humans to invest in gaining control. The Bible threatens self-determination by requiring us to hand over control of our lives to God. It is clear from the research that most individuals—

even a large majority of those who consider themselves to be Christian, and who participate in Christian activities—are unwilling to surrender the reins of their life to a God whom they do not personally know, understand or trust.

Top 10 Most Seductive Unbiblical Ideas Americans Adopt			
		Have Biblical Worldview?	
Summary description of unbiblical idea	All Adults	Yes	No
Believe in karma	57%	33%	58%
Having some faith matters more than which faith	62	42	62
Premarital sex between unmarried people who love each other is morally acceptable	74	4	77
Absolute moral truth does not exist	67	14	69
People are basically good	69	52	71
All religious faiths are of equal value	62	9	64
Most trusted personal source of moral guidance is something other than the Bible	69	4	71
Personal wealth is to be used to achieve outcomes other than advancing God's purposes	81	19	83
Success is about happiness, fulfillment, good health, higher consciousness, goodness, or productivity	79	2	82
People are not born into sin and therefore do not need to be saved by Jesus Christ	75	3	77
Source: *American Worldview Inventory 2021*, Cultural Research Center at Arizona Christian University; N=2,000 U.S. Adults, 2021.			

Consider a few of the examples that demonstrate the relationship of our drive for control with the underlying worldview people embrace. Accepting the principle of karma, believing that all faiths are equal or that any faith is acceptable, the rejection of moral absolutes, the ability to use wealth as desired—these are all examples of individuals seeking control rather than following biblical lifestyle admonitions.

Even believing that humans have the ability and authority to make unfettered moral choices gives individuals the perception of control.

Our desire to experience pleasure is the other seductive life view pointed to by the research. Several of the most seductive unbiblical worldviews focus on providing the individual with pleasure through sexual, material or relational means.

Biblical Christianity is not only about giving God control, but also about making choices that reflect His prescribed ways of life. That includes embracing brokenness, submission, surrender, sacrifice, and simplicity. That feels un-American these days, promoting an approach to life that is at odds with the American Dream, or certainly out of step with the constitutional guarantee of the right to happiness. (By the way, in case you were not paying careful attention, the Declaration of Independence doesn't speak of the right to happiness, but to the pursuit of happiness.)

CHAPTER 6

WHAT DOES IT MEAN WHEN PEOPLE SAY THEY ARE "CHRISTIAN"?

When someone says they are American, the meaning of that term is clear. Someone who claims to be a policeman leaves little doubt as to their job. But when people describe themselves as "Christian," what does that mean?

The meaning of "Christian" in America today is far from monolithic, with many diverse and often-conflicting theological views—even beliefs that are thoroughly unbiblical—among those embraced by people who claim the Christian name. Those differences in beliefs often lead to widely divergent beliefs and behaviors on matters of morality and politics among American Christians, depending on how closely and consistently they are aligned with basic biblical teachings.

One of our most surprising research findings is that the vast majority of American adults (69%) self-identifies as "Christian" and embraces many basic tenets of the faith. But a closer look shows that at the same time, many in this group hold views clearly in conflict with traditional biblical teachings. In fact, only 9% of U.S. adults who describe themselves as Christian possess a biblical worldview.

The tensions in terminology and the theological crosscurrents do not end there. There are many different segments of the population who claim to have some type of connection to Christianity. Among the segments within the larger group who call themselves Christian are: self-identified born-again Christians, self-described evangelical Christians, people whose theological beliefs establish them as born-again Christians, and people who possess a biblical worldview (referred to as Integrated Disciples). The differences in the belief and behavioral profiles of these groups are revealing.

Size of the Christian Universe

The first distinction that grabs one's attention is the dramatic range in the number of people who might be described as Christian, depending upon the definition used. The most inclusive definition is self-identification—people who simply say they are Christian—a group that currently stands at 69%. At the opposite end of the continuum are those who are deemed to be Christian by virtue of possessing a biblical worldview, a segment that encompasses a mere 6% of the adult population. The other three definitions examined in the study characterize anywhere from 28% to 35% of adults.

Applying those percentages to the aggregate U.S. adult population enables us to project the total head count of "Christians" to range from a high of an estimated 176 million self-professed Christians to a low of about 15 million adults who have a biblical worldview.

Self-Identified "Christian" Adults

Not surprisingly, the 69% of individuals who call themselves Christian is the largest of the various "Christian" segments evaluated and includes the broadest spectrum of theological points of view.

A large share of this population embraces various biblical principles and truths. For instance:

- 79% believe that God has a reason for everything.
- 77% say they have a unique, God-given calling.

- 74% say they intentionally try to avoid sinning because they know it hurts God.
- 72% claim that every moral choice either honors or dishonors God.
- 62% agree that the universe was designed and created, and is sustained by God.
- 61% believe that God is the all-knowing, all-powerful, perfect and just Creator of the universe who still rules the universe today.

We may celebrate the fact that considerable numbers of these people share some common beliefs, but it's important to not lose sight of the fact that a substantial number of people who claim the Christian label—ranging from two out of 10 to four out of 10—rejects these basic biblical beliefs. And just how mindboggling is it that four out of 10 self-proclaimed Christians *do not even believe in the God of the scriptures?*

But the flip side of the heresy coin is that a majority of self-proclaimed Christians endorse a wide range of perspectives that are not in harmony with biblical teachings. Among the wayward perspectives most widely embraced by self-identified Christians are:

- 72% argue that people are basically good.
- 71% consider feelings, experience, or the input of friends and family as their most trusted sources of moral guidance.
- 66% say that having faith matters more than which faith you adopt.
- 64% say that all religious faiths are of equal value.
- 58% believe that if a person is good enough, or does enough good things, they can earn their way into Heaven.
- 58% contend that the Holy Spirit is not a real, living being but is merely a symbol of God's power, presence or purity.

- 57% believe in karma.
- 52% claim that determining moral truth is up to each individual; there are no moral absolutes that apply to everyone, all the time.

How Many Adults Fall Within These Faith Categories?		
Description of the category	Percent of adults	Number of adults
Self-identified Christians	69%	176 million
Self-identified born-again Christians	35	89 million
Self-identified evangelical Christians	28	71 million
Theologically identified born-again Christians	28	71 million
Integrated Disciples – possess a biblical worldview	6	15 million
Source: *American Worldview Inventory 2021*, Cultural Research Center at Arizona Christian University; N=2,000 U.S. Adults, 2021.		

Large minorities of self-identified Christians are also likely to reject various biblical teachings and principles. For example, slightly less than half (46%) believe that the marriage of one man to one woman is God's plan for humanity, just 40% believe that when they die they will go to Heaven solely because they have confessed their sins and accepted Jesus Christ as their savior, only one-third (34%) believes that people are born into sin and can only be saved of the consequences by Jesus Christ, just one-third (32%) believes premarital sex is morally unacceptable, and about one out of every four (28%) believes that the best indicator of a successful life is consistent obedience to God.

This bizarre mixture of beliefs demonstrates why only 9% of self-identified Christians have a biblical worldview. The faith narrative driving the self-identified Christian population, then, is often out of sync with biblical perspectives. It might be articulated in this way:

> God is real, powerful, and caring. He/She is worthy of worship and consideration. He/She is open-minded and tolerant. Our moral choices are important but primarily because of their effect on other people rather than their consistency with God's principles and impact on our relationship with Him/Her. Those choices are best influenced by human experience and personal expectations. If we commit ourselves to being happy, God will bless those efforts because His goal is for us to be happy. Toward that end, the best advice to follow is the wisdom developed and shared by other people.

Self-Identified Born-Again Christians

Many polling organizations shortcut the spiritual classification process by simply asking people if they embrace a particular religious label (a process known as self-identification). One common measure along those lines is to ask people if they consider themselves to be born-again Christians. The typical range of people who fit this self-classification is 30% to 40%. The most recent Cultural Research Center estimate for this measure is 35%. This represents about half of the people who call themselves Christian.

How does this tighter definition of being a Christian (i.e., calling oneself born-again) differ theologically from the broader measure (i.e., those who simply describe themselves as Christian)? A majority of self-identified born-again Christians believes various principles taught in the Bible, including the following:

- 78% believe that the marriage of one man to one woman is God's plan for humanity, across all cultures.
- 72% believe that God is the all-knowing, all-powerful and

just Creator of the universe who still rules the universe today.

- 60% believe that the Bible is the accurate and reliable words of God.

But there are numerous views accepted by self-identified born-again Christians that conflict with biblical teachings:

- 77% say that having faith matters more than which faith you pursue.
- 69% accepted feelings, experience, and the input of friends and family as their most trusted sources of moral guidance.
- 65% say there is no absolute moral truth.
- 62% contend that the Holy Spirit is not a real, living being, but is merely a symbol of God's power, presence, or purity.
- 61% say that all religious faiths are of equal value.
- 60% believe that if a person is good enough, or does enough good things, they can earn their way into Heaven.

Interestingly, just 44% believe that when they die they will go to Heaven, but only because they have confessed their sins and accepted Jesus Christ as their savior. In other words, nearly six out of 10 people who claim to be born-again do not meet the widely accepted, biblical definition of born-again.

Overall, this segment is comprised of people who are somewhat more likely than those in the broader, self-identified "Christian" category to possess biblical perspectives. However, people in this segment are also likely to possess many unbiblical beliefs.

The grand faith narrative that characterizes self-described born-again Christians is a bit different from that of the more generic Christian category:

> God is real and powerful, as well as broad-minded, forgiving and tolerant. Sin is real but you can either earn salvation by being good enough or you may receive it through a grace-based relationship with Jesus Christ. Moral choices matter, but we are inevitably captives of karma. The Bible is a critical guide to life but it does not to contain absolute moral or comprehensive and indisputable spiritual truths. Consequently, the best sources of guidance are feelings, experience, and interpersonal advice.

Self-Identified Evangelical Christians

From a sociological standpoint, self-identified born-again Christians are the siblings of self-identified evangelicals. There is tremendous overlap between the two categories. In fact, roughly seven out of 10 consider themselves to be part of both segments. They are not interchangeable, though. There are slightly fewer self-identified evangelicals than self-identified born-again: 28% versus 35%, respectively.

Despite using different terminology to identify themselves, self-identified born-again and self-identified evangelical Christians possess nearly identical views on most of the beliefs evaluated. Across more than a dozen attributes studied, the average difference was only two percentage points, with the largest gap being only four percentage points.

Comparison of Religious Beliefs of Five "Christian" Segments					
	Self-identified			Theologically identified	
Belief	Christians	Born-again Christians	Evangelical Christian	Born-again	Integrated Disciples
Bible is the accurate, reliable word of God	52%	60%	58%	74%	99+%
Determining moral truth is up to each individual; there are no moral absolutes that apply to everyone, all the time	52	65	65	40	25
God is the all-powerful, all-knowing, perfect and just creator of the universe who rules that universe today	61	72	69	83	99+
Having faith matters more than which faith you have	66	77	74	56	42
Your most trusted, primary source of moral guidance is your feelings, experiences, or advice from friends and family	71	69	65	54	4
A person who is generally good, or does enough good things for others, will earn a place in Heaven	58	60	61	37	5
Source: Cultural Research Center at Arizona Christian University; N=5,000 adults 18 or older, nationally representative sample.					

Theologically Identified Born-Again Christians

Slightly less than three out of every 10 American adults (28%) currently qualify as a born-again Christian based upon their theological perspective.

One might expect those who call themselves "born-again" and those whose theological positions place them in the "born-again" category to be very similar. They are not.

"Theologically identified born-again Christians" are described as such because they believe that when they die, they will go to Heaven, but only because they have confessed their sins and accepted Jesus Christ as their savior. Overall, one-third of those who qualify as born-again based on their theological views (31%) do not embrace the term "born-again" to describe themselves. Similarly, among those who consider themselves to be born-again, 57% do not qualify for that term theologically.

The decision to rely upon Jesus Christ as their savior is definitely a game-changer—not just in terms of eternal destiny but also related to earth-bound choices. Compared to the self-identified born-again believers, the theologically defined group is substantially *more* likely to believe the following:

- 84% believe that God is the all-knowing, all-powerful and just Creator of the universe who still rules the universe today.
- 74% believe that the Bible is the accurate and reliable words of God.

Continuing the comparison, theologically defined born-again adults are significantly less likely than self-identified born-again believers to adopt counter-biblical beliefs, such as the following:

- 56% say that having faith matters more than which faith you pursue.

- 54% accept feelings, experience and the input of friends and family as their most trusted sources of moral guidance.
- 51% say that all religious faiths are of equal value.
- 50% contend that the Holy Spirit is not a real, living being but is merely a symbol of God's power, presence or purity.
- 40% say there is no absolute moral truth.
- 37% believe that if a person is good enough, or does enough good things, they can earn their way into Heaven.
- 31% believe that the Bible is ambiguous in its teaching about abortion.

Notice, however, although the theologically identified segment features a larger proportion of members who are aligned with biblical perspectives on a substantial number of beliefs, most of the theologically defined born-again group holds some views that contradict biblical teaching. Among the most pervasive examples include: rejection of the exclusivity of Christianity; denying the Bible as their primary source of moral guidance; accepting other faiths as being of equal value to Christianity; deeming the embrace of some religious faith to be more important than which faith they embrace; and not believing in the existence of the Holy Spirit.

The theologically defined born-again group is the most likely of the four segments examined thus far to reflect biblical perspectives, yet only 19% the group has a biblical worldview.

Integrated Disciples: The Biblical Worldview Cohort

As our *American Worldview Inventory* surveys demonstrate, just 6% of U.S. adults possess a biblical worldview. Labeled "Integrated Disciples" for their demonstrated ability to assimilate their beliefs into their lifestyle, this group consistently—albeit imperfectly—comes closest to reflecting biblical principles into their opinions, beliefs, behaviors, and preferences.

When it comes to social, moral, and political issues, Integrated Disciples tend to be more conservative than other self-identified Christians.

Compared to the other four "Christian" segments, individuals holding the biblical worldview are more likely to possess biblical beliefs regarding a range of issues:

- 99+% believe that the Bible is the accurate and reliable words of God.
- 99+% believe that God is the all-knowing, all-powerful, perfect and just creator of the universe who still rules the universe today.
- 99+% say they have a unique, God-given calling.
- 99+% say they intentionally try to avoid sinning because they know it hurts God.
- 96% claim that every moral choice either honors or dishonors God.
- 88% believe that God has a reason for everything.

And while they are not in perfect unison with the scriptures on some issues, only small minorities of Integrated Disciples—less than one out of every 10—hold unscriptural positions on a variety of matters such as:

- 4% accept feelings, experience, and the input of friends and family as their most trusted sources of moral guidance.
- 5% believe that if a person is good enough, or does enough good things, they can earn their way into Heaven.
- 8% believe that the Bible is ambiguous in its teaching about abortion.
- 9% say that all religious faiths are of equal value.

Still, shockingly large numbers of Integrated Disciples stray from biblical principles by embracing the following beliefs:

- 25% say there is no absolute moral truth.
- 33% believe in karma.
- 39% contend that the Holy Spirit is not a real, living being but is merely a symbol of God's power, presence or purity.
- 42% believe that having faith matters more than which faith you pursue.
- 52% argue that people are basically good.

These theological glitches in the worldview of Integrated Disciples underscore our experience that very few have a pure or biblically perfect worldview. Those whom we categorize as Integrated Disciples are not faultless replicas of Jesus Christ. They are simply the segment of the population that thinks and acts like Jesus in at least four out of every five instances. They are the people who are the most Christ-like among us, but they, too, have rough edges and need spiritual growth and refinement.

Lifestyle Implications

Each of the "Christian" segments stakes out divergent positions on political and moral matters. Here are a few examples of those differences.

2020 Presidential Vote

Just one out of five Integrated Disciples (20%) voted for Joe Biden in the 2020 election. That was less than half as many who voted for President Biden among self-identified born-again (41%), self-identified evangelicals (43%), and self-identified Christians (46%). In between the ends of the continuum was the theologically identified born-again group, of which 30% voted for the Democrat.

Interestingly, none of the Christian segments featured a majority voting for Joe Biden. His ultimate victory was the result of a broad array of non-Christian segments—Jews, Muslims, adherents of Eastern religions, other non-Christian faith groups and the irreligious—supporting him by substantial margins, exploiting the division within the "Christian" vote.

Election Media Coverage

Only one out of five Integrated Disciples (20%) viewed media coverage of the 2020 Election as fair and objective. Slightly less than half of the theologically determined born-again segment (48%) held that view. However, a substantial majority felt the coverage was fair and objective among self-identified Christians (61%), self-identified born-again adults (65%), and self-identified evangelicals (66%).

Social Issues

The most contentious issues in political elections tend to be those categorized as social issues: e.g., abortion, gay rights, gun policy, environmental protection, law and order, immigration laws, etc. The various segments of Christians hold distinctly different places on the ideological spectrum concerning social issues.

Self-identified Christians were the group most likely to claim liberal or progressive positions on social issues, although just one-third of them (32%) embraced that ideology, compared to 42% from the same group that identified as conservative.

The other pair of self-identified segments—the self-identified born-again Christians and the self-identified evangelical Christians—were much more likely to say they were conservative than to label themselves liberal or progressive regarding social issues. Just more than one-quarter of each segment identified as liberal on social issues, while roughly half of each group claimed to be socially conservative.

The theologically identified born-again Christians were two-and-a-half times more likely to self-identify as conservative than liberal/progressive.

In four out of five cases, Integrated Disciples were in the conservative camp. Only one out of every 20 of them identified as liberal/progressive.

Moral Choices

The *American Worldview Inventory 2021* discovered that moral behaviors vary according to the individual's Christian niche, too. For instance, self-identified Christians are barely half as likely as Integrated Disciples to contend that lying—described in the survey as "telling a falsehood of minor consequence in order to protect their personal best interests or reputation"—is morally unacceptable.

Similarly, Integrated Disciples were about twice as likely as self-identified Christians to consider aborting an unborn child in a case where "having an abortion because their partner has left and the parent knows they cannot reasonably take care of the child"—to be morally unacceptable.

The Different Christian Segments Have Divergent Ideological Positions on Social Issues

Description of the category	Liberal	Moderate	Conservative
Self-identified Christians	32%	26%	42%
Self-identified born-again Christians	28	27	45
Self-identified evangelical Christians	27	23	50
Theologically identified born-again Christians	23	20	57
Integrated Disciples – possess a biblical worldview	5	13	82

Source: National research conducted by the Cultural Research Center at Arizona Christian University. N=5,000 adults 18 or older, nationally representative sample.

"Having sexual relations with someone that you love and expect to marry in the future" was considered morally unacceptable to three times as many Integrated Disciples as self-identified Christians.

While six out of 10 self-identified Christians deemed "declaring small tax deductions you are not eligible for, but will not be discovered by the IRS, to lower your tax bill" to be morally unacceptable—substantially less than the nearly unanimous rejection of that behavior among Integrated Disciples.

In each situation surveyed, the proportion of theologically defined born-again Christians who rejected the behavior was roughly halfway between that of the self-identified Christians and the Integrated Disciples.

Morally Unacceptable Behaviors According to Different Christian Segments				
Description of the category	Lying	Abortion	Unmarried Sex	Tax Cheating
Self-identified Christians	53%	55%	32%	59%
Theologically Identified born-again Christians	67	72	51	71
Integrated Disciples – possess a biblical worldview	99+	98	97	99+
Source: National research conducted by the Cultural Research Center at Arizona Christian University. N=5,000 adults 18 or older, nationally representative sample.				

Socialism

When asked if they would prefer socialism or capitalism, three out of 10 self-identified Christians (29%) favored socialism. About four out of 10 of the other self-identified segments—the self-identified born-again Christians (37%) and the self-identified evangelical Christians (40%)—noted a preference for socialism. Just two out of 10 of the theologically-identified born-again Christians (21%) opted for socialism. By far the least likely advocates of the Marxist approach were Integrated Disciples: a paltry 4% of them favored socialism to capitalism.

Guidance on Taking Up the Name of Christ

It's one thing to call yourself a fan of a sports team or a devotee of a particular brand. It's something else altogether to call yourself by the name of the savior of humankind.

Jesus spoke to this issue in what is known as the Sermon on the Mount. During that exposition He admonished people to claim to be one of His followers only if they were consistently applying His principles in their life.

> Not everyone who calls out to me, "Lord! Lord!" will enter the Kingdom of Heaven. Only those who actually do the will of my Father in heaven will enter. On judgment day many will say to me, "Lord! Lord! We prophesied in your name and cast out demons in your name and performed many miracles in your name." But I will reply, "I never knew you. Get away from me, you who break God's laws." (Matthew 7:21-23, NLT)

Obedience is of paramount importance to Jesus. He noted that a person would be His disciple if they obey His teachings (John 8:31). It follows, then, that when a person takes on the name "Christian" it refers to one who is striving to know and follow the teachings and example of Jesus Christ.

That is not always the case in contemporary America.

Too often, people who are simply religious, or regular churchgoers, or perhaps want a certain reputation or image, embrace the label "Christian," regardless of their spiritual life and intentions. "Christian" has become somewhat of a generic term rather than a name that reflects a deep commitment to passionately pursuing and being like Jesus Christ.

Americans have become sloppy regarding their spiritual perceptions and definitions. That makes it all the more important that we be very careful when interpreting data associated with a particular segment of people who are labeled as or have appropriated the designation "Christian." Political polling, in particular, may mislead people regarding the views and preferences of genuine Christ-followers with those who are Christian in name only, simply based on how those surveys measure the Christian population—and how the term "Christian" is defined.

CHAPTER 7

THE NATIONAL RELIGIOUS REALIGNMENT: DRAMATIC CHANGES IN LONG-TERM FAITH COMMITMENTS

One of the defining strengths of America for more than two centuries has been the consistency of people's faith commitments. Not only did more than nine out of 10 Americans associate with the same faith (Christianity), that alignment brought with it consensual views about morality, purpose, family, lifestyle, citizenship, and values. The dramatic erosion of shared Christian belief over the past 30 years has ushered in many rapid and radical changes to the relatively stable religious alignments of the nation.

Several major shifts in the U.S. religious landscape have notably changed the spiritual profile of America.

- There have been dramatic changes in the faith of American Hispanics. Those include a decrease in the number of Hispanic Catholics, as well as a sharp increase in Hispanic "Don'ts"—those who don't believe, don't know, or don't care if God exists.
- There has been rapid growth in the Islamic faith, as well as Eastern and New Age religions.
- The past 30 years has produced a precipitous decline in both the number of self-identified Christians and in people's confidence in religion as an answer to their needs.

- The United States has sustained a breathtaking drop in four critical spiritual indicators: belief in God, belief in the Bible, seeking eternal salvation through a relationship with and forgiveness through Jesus Christ, and personal possession of a biblical worldview.
- Belief in reincarnation, even among Christians, has risen dramatically in a short period of time.

Hispanic Faith

Hispanics became the plurality of immigrants during the 1980s and have emerged as the majority of immigrants each year starting in the late 1990s. Hispanics represented one out of every five immigrants entering the United States in 1960, but have been more than half of all immigrants each year for the past three-plus decades.[1]

A large majority of the Hispanic community has traditionally described themselves as Catholic. For the past several decades, in particular, Hispanics have been a major growth segment for the Catholic Church in America. But as Hispanics have succumbed to the same acculturation pressures as the rest of the population, their church loyalty has plummeted.

An examination of the church affiliation of Hispanics shows that their relationship to Catholicism is rapidly shifting. In 1991, 59% of Hispanics in the United States self-identified as Catholics.[2] That figure dropped a bit over the next decade, declining to 54% in 2001. However, there was nearly double the level of decline over the following decade, dipping below the 50-percent mark to just 45% in 2011. An even more substantial drop has occurred in the past 10 years, falling to just 28% in 2021. In other words, the proportion of Hispanic adults in the United States who claim to be Catholic has been sliced in half—from 59% to 28%—in the last 30 years.

As Hispanics leave the Catholic faith, where are they going? While there has been a minor uptick in alignments with non-Christian faiths, those allegiances reflect only about one out of 10 Hispanics (9%). And the nearly 300 Protestant denominations in America have generally failed to attract wayward Hispanic Catholics, with Protestant adherence among Hispanics dropping slightly since 2001, from 35% in 2001 to just 32% in 2021.

The big gains have been among the "Don'ts"—i.e., people who say they don't know, don't care or don't believe that God exists. A mere 3% of Hispanics fell into the Don'ts category in 1991, but that tripled by 2001 to 9%. That number grew by another one-third over the next decade (12% in 2011), and then exploded to nearly one-third of Hispanics by 2021 (31%). That means the proportion of Don'ts among Hispanics has grown tenfold in the last three decades.

The Shifting Religious Allegiances of Hispanics				
Faith Affiliation	1991	2001	2011	2021
Catholic	59%	54%	45%	28%
Protestant	30	35	37	32
Non-Christian faith	8	2	6	9
Don'ts	3	9	12	31
Source: *American Worldview Inventory* 2021, Cultural Research Center at Arizona Christian University; N=2,000 U.S. Adults, 2021. OmniPoll™ (1991, 2001, 2011), Barna Group, Ventura, CA.				

Fastest-growing Religious Faiths

The expansion of the Don'ts among Hispanics is indicative of how rapidly that segment is growing across all of America. Only one out of 10 U.S. adults fit in that category in 1991 and again 10 years later in 2001. The segment nudged up by just a couple more percentage points by 2011. That means most of the incredible growth of that category has taken place in the past decade, with the number of Don'ts nationwide nearly tripling from 12% in 2011 to 34% in 2021.

Who is responsible for that rapid and substantial growth? As described above, Hispanics are one major growth segment. Another leading segment is the Millennial generation (people between the ages of 18 and 36 at the time of the survey). The *AWVI 2021* showed that 43% of Millennials are Don'ts—the highest of any adult generation in the country.

Other population segments gravitating faster than the norm toward questioning or rejecting the existence of God include: political liberals (49%), people who are not registered to vote (40%), and residents of the Northeast (40%) or California (40%). Not surprisingly, above-average levels of people who draw heavily from non-biblical worldviews also qualify as Don'ts—i.e., those who often rely on Marxism (58%), Nihilism (70%), Secular Humanism (85%), and Postmodernism (87%).

But the research also identified two other rapidly growing faith segments. One of those is Islam. While the Muslim faith had virtually no presence in the United States prior to the early 1990s (less than one-half of one percent of adults affiliated with Islam in 1991), that proportion has jumped in the past decade to nearly 3%. Granted, that percentage is small in comparison to several other faith groups. But the growth rate of Islam in America has exceeded even that of the Don'ts during the last decade. And the suddenness with which that growth has taken place is also worth noting.

In addition, Eastern religions (such as Buddhism and Hinduism) have also experienced a resurgence in recent years. Presently, nearly 5% of American adults associate with an Eastern or New Age religion. That is more than double the proportion measured a decade ago and is indicative of the magnitude of the current search for alternatives to Christianity. Some of that increase is also attributable to the continued expansion of the Asian population in America, now estimated to exceed 5% of the aggregate population.[3] That growth is related to changes in immigration patterns, which has seen an explosion in Asian immigration in the United

States. In 1960, immigrants from Asia were 5% of the total immigrant pool; in 2019, immigrants from Asian nations had risen to 31% of all incoming immigrants.[4]

It seems obvious that changes in immigration patterns within the United States in recent years have significantly contributed to the rise of alternative faiths in the country—and to the heightened disinterest in Christianity.

Christianity's Status Has Changed

So where does Christianity stand in the religious mix of the nation? More than nine out of 10 Americans claimed to be Christians as recently as 1980. Since that time there has been a steady erosion of self-identification with the nation's foundational faith. By 1990 the proportion had dropped to eight out of 10. That level remained consistent until after the turn of the millennium, when the decline began to gain momentum. By 2010 three out of four adults claimed to be Christian. Currently, roughly two out of three make the same claim.

Confidence in religion has shown a corresponding decline during that period. In the 1970s two-thirds of Americans had a high level of confidence in religion. The decline in such confidence began in the mid-1980s—the same time that the notable drop in alignment with Christianity started. By 2000 confidence in religion had fallen to 56%. And the drop has continued to this day, with barely four out of 10 adults professing to have a high degree of confidence in religion.

Perhaps the most telling reflection of the decline of Christianity as the preferred faith in America is demonstrated by the concurrent declines in a quartet of faith-related measures that the author has been tracking since the late 1970s. The shift in people's answers to these measures is breathtaking.

- Belief in the existence of God as the all-knowing, all-powerful creator of the universe who still rules the world today—from 86% in 1991 to 46% in 2021.[5]
- Belief that the Bible is the accurate and reliable word of God—from 70% in 1991 to 41% in 2021.
- Belief that upon death the respondent will go to Heaven only because they have confessed their sins and accepted Jesus Christ as their savior—36% in 1991 to 25% in 2021.
- Possess a biblical worldview—from 12% in 1995 to 6% in 2021.

Significant Changes in Four Critical Spiritual Indicators				
Indicator	1991	2001	2011	2021
Hold an orthodox, biblical view of God	86%	72%	67%	46%
Believe the Bible is the accurate word of God	70	60	62	41
Believe they will go to heaven soley due to confession of sins, acceptance of Jesus Christ as their personal savior	36	41	39	30
Possess a biblical worldview	12	n/a	n/a	6
Source: *American Worldview Inventory 2021*, Cultural Research Center at Arizona Christian University; N=2,000 U.S. Adults, 2021. OmniPoll™ (1991, 2001, 2011), Barna Group, Ventura, CA.				

Life After Death

The data described above point to the decline in the proportion of Americans who can be described as born-again Christians based on their beliefs (as opposed to the unreliable estimates based upon self-identification, as discussed in the previous chapter). During the past three decades, that statistic has plummeted from a high of 45% to the current 28%.[6]

If Americans are less inclined to embrace Jesus Christ as their savior and rely on their admission and confession of sins and His grace for their salvation, what do they believe about life after death?

One of the most surprising shifts has been the renewed interest in reincarnation. After a flirtation with that belief in the Psychedelic '70s, reincarnation barely registered as possible eternal outcome in national surveys throughout the 1990s and early 2000s. However, the past decade has given rise to a new following for Eastern religious thought and practices, perhaps sparked by yoga, meditation, the "mindfulness movement," and the greater accessibility to information about Eastern beliefs and practices facilitated by new technologies.

Currently, 9% of adults believe they will be reincarnated. That proportion is likely to continue growing, given the twin engines of a decline in Christian beliefs and the fact that four out of 10 Americans (39%) believe that reincarnation is "a real possibility" for them. The potential for continued growth in the acceptance of reincarnation is further advanced by that possibility being heavily supported by several key population segments:

- LGBTQ adults, who are among the most influence-driven segments (65%).
- The fastest-growing racial group, Hispanics (54%).
- The youngest adults, the Millennials (51%).
- Parents of young children (47%).
- Liberals, currently the most politically potent ideological segment (47%).
- Residents of our largest states, which have greater influence on the nation (43%).

Amazingly, substantial proportions of people associated with Christianity embrace the possibility of reincarnation. For instance, one out of four (24%) theologically identified born-again Christians accept reincarnation as a possibility. Don't overlook just how mind-blowing that statistic is: people who acknowledge their sins, and ask God through Christ to forgive them, nevertheless say they may come back as some other life form rather than reside eternally in God's presence! In addition, more than one-third of all self-identified Christians (36%) also believe that reincarnation is a real possibility for them.

It is relevant to point out that Americans generally reject the idea of going to Hell or some place of eternal torment, after their time on earth expires. Currently, just 2% of Americans believe they will experience Hell after they die. That figure has stayed remarkably stable over the last 40 years, fluctuating between 1% and 2% throughout that entire period.

Restoring Christian Vitality

If you sit back and ponder these changes, you cannot conclude it's "life as usual" in America. A genuine leader, faced with these trends, would recommend that our nation's ministry leaders consider a new mindset and approach to Christian ministry in America.

In fact, the data point out that with an estimated 180 million adults (and perhaps an additional 60 to 70 million children and teens) who are not born-again, the United States has become one of the largest and most important mission fields in the world. Our young-adult population, in particular, is abandoning long-established faith patterns. They do not embrace many of the core beliefs and behaviors that characterized those who came before them.

The emerging America is radically different—demographically, politically, relationally, and spiritually. It is a young, non-white, mobile population. This group is largely indifferent to the well-being of the United States, and is demonstrably skeptical of the nation's history, foundations, traditions, and ways of life. They are technologically advanced, sexually unrestrained, emotionally unpredictable, and a spiritual hybrid.

It's becoming increasingly clear that Christian ministry as practiced for the past five decades will not be effective with this unique population.

Worldview and faith maturity statistics also make quite clear that those ministry practices have also been largely ineffective during those past five decades.

Leading the nation to a place of comprehensive spiritual and moral health will depend on how we shape the worldview of our people. Because a worldview is developed when people are young (i.e., under the age of 13), it is imperative that Christian ministries, led by our numerous churches, focus on and invest most heavily in reaching children with biblical truth and equipping their parents to be significant contributors in that effort. And because the Bible is increasingly rejected as a trustworthy and relevant document of life principles, we must re-establish the reasons for its value and reliability.

Given that most young Americans view life success as whatever produces happiness or satisfaction, we will have to address the emptiness and inadequacies of a life devoted to self and satisfying our fickle and fluid emotions. Without a solid foundation of truth upon which choices can be made, a society is doomed to hardships, failures and conflict. In the person of Jesus Christ and through the pages of the Bible, absolute moral truths are knowable and can be applied to facilitate a successful and meaningful life.

If we were objective and honest, we would acknowledge that many of the approaches now relied upon by Christian ministries—and especially by churches—are inadequate to impact the emerging population that needs to be reached with God's truths and principles.

It's unlikely our typical church services and programs will effectively minister to people in the way they did in the distant past. Reconsidering what it takes to make disciples in such a different environment is a necessary step toward re-establishing church life as transformational. For many decades, global missionaries have lived by the creed of understanding the foreign culture they have moved into and adapting their practices without compromising biblical principles. That missionary mindset is needed in the United States today.

As our nation navigates this period of societal chaos and turbulence, allowing Christian leaders the freedom to radically but intelligently re-imagine new ministry strategies and tactics will be a necessary step toward helping America return to Christ.

NOTES:

1. Abby Budiman, Christine Tamire, Lauren Mora, and Luis Noe-Bustamante, "Facts on U.S. Immigrants, 2018," Pew Research Center, August 20, 2020. https://www.pewresearch.org/hispanic/2020/08/20/facts-on-u-s-immigrants/. See also: Migration Policy Institute (MPI) tabulation of data from U.S. Census Bureau, 2010 and 2019 American Community Surveys (ACS), and 2000 Decennial Census; data for 1960 to 1990 were from Campbell J. Gibson and Emily Lennon, "Historical Census Statistics on the Foreign-Born Population of the United States: 1850-1990" (Working Paper No. 29, U.S. Census Bureau, Washington D.C., February 1999).
2. All facts about religion among Hispanics in America come from the Barna Group (www.barna.com) and the Cultural Research Center at Arizona Christian University (www.CulturalResearchCenter.com).
3. Abby Budiman and Neil G. Ruiz, "Key facts about Asian Americans, a diverse and growing population," Pew Research Center, April 29, 2021, https://www.pewresearch.org/fact-tank/2021/04/29/key-facts-about-asian-americans/.
4. Ibid.
5. This measured as high as 45% during this three-decade span and was 39% in 2011 (see Chapter 6).
6. This measurement does not use the term "born-again" in the survey question. We often refer to this as a measurement of "theologically identified born-again Christians" as differentiated from "self-described born-again Christians" (see Chapter 6).

CHAPTER 8

THE SEISMIC GENERATIONAL SHIFT IN WORLDVIEW: MILLENNIALS SEEK A NATION WITHOUT GOD, THE BIBLE, AND CHURCHES

Perhaps the most alarming of our research findings is to see how far the nation's youngest adults—the Millennials[1]—have shifted away from the biblical worldview.

The Millennial generation has a lot going for it. They are technologically savvy, highly educated, active in community affairs, and highly influential in the marketplace. Add to that their prolific size—the most populous adult generation in the nation today—and it is evident that they will be shaping the nature of America for years to come. Clearly, cultural momentum is on their side.

But there is an important difference between capacity and competence. Yes, the generation has the resources to redefine life as we know it. But will they make the best choices in that process? If the alarming shift in their worldview—the combination of their spiritual beliefs and related life practices—is any indication, the nation is in for a tumultuous ride into a murky future.

The concern is not that Millennials (ages 18 to 36 at the time of the survey) aspire to a different life experience than do their predecessors. More so, the apprehensions of older adults relate to the foundations on which our youngest adult generation appears poised to base the pursuit of their cultural ideals.

Common Threads

One point of commonality is that the dominant worldview of all four adult generations in the United States is Syncretism—the mash-up of various worldviews held by nine out of 10 adults that provides everyone with a customized understanding of and response to life. A large majority of each generation relies on a syncretistic worldview when making their life choices. Overall, 89% of Millennials, 86% of Gen Xers, 83% of Boomers, and 86% of Builders reflect Syncretism as their dominant worldview.[1]

The breadth of acceptance of Syncretism means that none of those four generations has even one out of 10 members accepting as their dominant philosophy of life one of the seven definable, well-known worldviews we studied—Biblical Theism, Moralistic Therapeutic Deism, Postmodernism, Secular Humanism, Eastern Mysticism, Marxism, or Nihilism.

The failure to embrace a biblical worldview is evident even though a majority of Americans, regardless of their generation, consider themselves to be Christian. Self-identification with the Christian faith ranged from a low of 57% of Millennials to a high of 83% among Builders (people in their late 70s or older).

Another shared trait across generations is that their worldview is most likely to depart from biblical principles regarding beliefs about the existence and source of truth; the reliability and relevance of the Bible; and the moral choices we make from day to day. Each of our four adult generations is moving, albeit at different speeds and toward divergent outcomes, away from historically embraced, scriptural teachings. That movement is perhaps masked by the fact that large numbers of people in each generation remain active in the life of Christian churches.

In the end, we also found that there were more than a dozen foundational biblical beliefs accepted by only a minority of members of each of the four adult generations. In other words, none of our four adult generations lack a biblical worldview because they have rejected just a few core beliefs and behaviors. Each generation has adopted a way of life that is at serious odds with biblical teachings.

Let's take a closer look at where each generation has gone off the rails.

Millennials Stand Apart

Despite these things in common with earlier generations, only 4% of Millennials possess a biblical worldview. Unsurprisingly, this results in the youngest adults diverging most significantly from scriptural precepts.

There are more than *two dozen* examples of Millennials being substantially more likely than any other generation to reject biblical principles in favor of more worldly spiritual perspectives and practices. Millennials, defined as people born between 1984 and 2002, i.e., aged 18 to 36 at the time of the survey, were far ***more likely*** than any other generation to:

- Define success in life as happiness, personal freedom, or productivity without oppression.
- Consider an abortion performed to reduce personal economic or emotional discomfort to be morally acceptable.
- Consider premarital sex with someone expected to be their future spouse to be morally acceptable.
- Deem reincarnation a real possibility.

- Self-identify as ideologically "liberal" regarding fiscal and social public policies.
- Champion liberal theology.
- Be among the "Don'ts"—people who do not know if God exists, do not believe He exists, or do not care if He exists.

Millennials were also much ***less likely*** than older Americans to hold other positions, such as:

- Being deeply committed to practicing their religious faith.
- Believing that the universe was designed, created, and is maintained by God.
- Believing that human beings were created by God, in His image, but are undermined by personal sin and therefore need to be redeemed through Jesus Christ.
- Accepting the idea of "original sin."
- Agreeing that the common purpose of humanity is to know, love, and serve God with all of our heart, mind, strength, and soul.
- Embracing the Bible as their primary source of moral guidance.
- Believing that every moral choice we make either honors or dishonors God.
- Accepting the notion of God being the all-knowing, all-powerful, and just creator of the universe who still rules that universe today.
- Considering Satan to be a real and influential being.

- Participating in religious activities such as:
    - worshipping God.
    - praying to God.
    - studying the Bible.
    - seeking and following God's will.
    - asking for God's forgiveness for their sins.
- Identifying as a Christian.
- Believing that after they die, they will spend eternity in God's presence solely because they have confessed their sins and have accepted Jesus Christ as their savior.

A comparison of generational responses to traditional measures of faith underscores the new approach to faith and morality practiced by Millennials. For example, while four out of 10 people 55 or older (40%) can be classified as theologically defined born-again Christians (i.e., categorized as such based on their beliefs about personal salvation), far fewer Gen X adults (26%) fit within the segment, but just one out of every six Millennials (16%) meets the criterion.

In contrast, while slightly more than one out of four Boomers and Builders (28%) qualify as "Don'ts"—that is, people who do not know, believe, or care if God exists—and roughly the same proportion of Gen X adults can be characterized as such (31%), closer to half of all Millennials (43%) are Don'ts.

But those spiritual transitions represent a continuation of dramatic changes introduced by Gen X prior to the arrival of the Millennials. The reshaping of America's religious landscape began nearly 60 years ago. Baby Boomers were the most aggressive initiators of spiritual change, embracing dramatically different beliefs and behaviors than their predecessors. Their successors, Gen X, realigned the nation's religious boundaries even further. The youngest adult generation of today—Millennials—is now threatening to reshape the nation's religious parameters beyond recognition.

Gen X Plus Millennials

Together, Gen Xers and Millennials (i.e., generations encompassing people currently in their late teens through mid-50s) emerged with many beliefs that stand in sharp contrast to those held by Boomers and Builders (the two generations representing people presently in their mid-50s and older). The younger pair of generations is substantially ***more likely*** than their elders to believe the following:

- Horoscopes provide useful guidance for their life.
- Getting even with those who offend or harm them is defensible.
- God is not involved in people's lives.
- Allowing people to own property facilitates economic injustice.
- Karma is a viable life principle.
- The Bible is ambiguous in what it teaches about abortion.
- Human beings have developed over a long period of time from less advanced life forms to our current condition.
- The Bible is not the accurate and reliable (i.e., inerrant) word of God.

In addition, the two younger adult generations are considerably *more likely* than older generations to rely primarily on Moralistic Therapeutic Deism for worldview guidance. They are also significantly *more likely* than people from older generations to argue that traditional moral perspectives are irrelevant today, considering an entire series of formerly rejected behaviors to be morally acceptable. Those included lying, not repaying loans, taking illegal tax deductions, speeding, committing suicide, or allowing for euthanasia.

On the other hand, the two younger generations are also much *less likely* than their older counterparts to accept the Golden Rule (i.e., treat others as you want them to treat you), to believe that wealth is provided by God for its possessors to manage for His purposes, or to believe that the universe was created without any divine intervention in that process.

A Brave New Millennial World

The results of the generational worldview analysis offer a stunning portrait of the world through the eyes of each generation. Millennials clearly have gone further than any recent generation in cutting ties with traditional Christian views and normative biblical teaching.

The research helps us to describe the kind of world that the attitudes, values, beliefs, and behaviors of Millennials would create. It includes these seven components:

1. Government would continue to expand in reach, authority, power, and spending, in order to facilitate a more desirable and comfortable way of living.
2. Public policies and programs would be more flexible and fluid. The syncretistic worldview they possess would produce a less predictable and less consistent society than has been the case in America's recent history. That unreliability would be a result of the inherently contradictory worldview positions adopted by Americans and the Millennial reliance upon feelings rather than facts to facilitate decisions.
3. There would be more episodes of violence and combativeness across the nation. Such outbursts would be

attributable to the Millennials' self-righteousness, sense of personal sovereignty, their dismissal of the legitimacy of institutional authority, their unwillingness to compromise, and feeling that not getting their way is a personal threat or challenge.

4. Political tensions would remain significant in the short-term due to their ambiguous national vision; disdain for compromise; their aggressive recalibration of morals and values; and their acceptance of a significantly revised history of our nation.
5. The Christian community would be smaller in numbers, less influential, and less economically robust thanks to acts of religious persecution and the elimination of numerous religious liberties. The changes resulting from the reshaping of America's religious alignment would include fewer people and less money being devoted to global Christian missions, and the withdrawal of existing privileges received by churches, such as tax and land-use exceptions.
6. Interpersonal relationships would be more difficult to sustain due to declining levels of interpersonal trust, the diminished willingness of young adults to find common ground and progress through compromise, a heightened reliance upon technology for communication, and personal disappointments produced by the lack of moral agreement.
7. Our nation's family units would be overhauled, producing a new profile of family relationships. This reshaping would emerge based on fewer formal marriages, proportionally increased levels of divorce, liberalized sexual morality, and the reduced appeal of having and raising children.

Generational Transitions in Significant Beliefs and Behaviors				
Belief or Behavior	Mill	GenX	Boom	Builder
Willing to try anything at least once	66%	57%	31%	28%
Believe in karma	64	61	32	30
Humans developed over time from less advanced forms	54	53	40	34
Reincarnation is a very real possibility	51	39	29	20
Personally receive guidance from your horoscope	35	32	10	3
Individual ownership of property facilitates economic injustice	35	34	13	16
You try to get even with people who have wronged you	38	33	12	10
Universal purpose for all people is to know, love, and serve God with all heart, mind, strength, and soul	19	30	42	60
Universe was designed and created, and is sustained by God	30	47	62	67
God is the all-knowing. all powerful, just creator of the universe; He still rules it today	31	47	57	64
Human beings were created by God in His image but are Fallen creatures in need of redemption by Jesus Christ	40	57	65	60
Satan is a real, influential being	44	58	64	55
Deeply committed to practicing my faith	45	57	64	72
You treat others as you want them to treat you	48	53	81	90

Source: *American Worldview Inventory 2021*, Cultural Research Center at Arizona Christian University; N=2,000 U.S. Adults, 2021. Note: Due to space limitations the descriptions above are not the exact wording used in the survey. Generation abbreviations and definitions: Mill = Millennials - born 1984-2002; Gen X = Generation X - born 1965-1983; Boom = Baby Boomers - born 1946-1964; Builders - born 1927-1945.

Generational Differences in Spirituality				
Spiritual Indicator	Mill	GenX	Boom	Builder
Consider yourself to be a Christian	57%	70%	79%	83%
Praise. thank, or worship God each week	45	66	70	72
Don't know, care, or believe that God exists	43	31	28	27
Believe that when they die they will go to Heaven but only because they confessed their sins and accepted Jesus Christ as their savior	16	26	41	39
Possesses a biblical worldview	4	6	8	9
Worldviews Heavily Relied Upon				
Moralistic Therapeutic Deism	44	38	32	29
Biblical Theism	9	22	42	47
Postmodernism	18	13	14	17
Secular Humanism	15	11	14	19
Eastern Mysticism	12	7	9	6
Nihilism	11	8	8	13
Marxism	10	9	9	14

Source: *American Worldview Inventory 2021*, Cultural Research Center at Arizona Christian University; N=2,000 U.S. Adults, 2021. Note: Due to space limitations the descriptions above are not the exact wording used in the survey. Generation abbreviations and definitions: Mill = Millennials - born 1984-2002; Gen X = Generation X - born 1965-1983; Boom = Baby Boomers - born 1946-1964; Builders - born 1927-1945.

Reshaping the World

Intentional or not, Gen X and Millennials have already solidified dramatic changes in the nation's central beliefs and lifestyles, with much more to come. From a nationwide perspective, the Christian Church has done shockingly little to push back against such dramatic challenges. Consequently, the societal influence of the Christian Church has diminished while the influence of three sectors in particular—arts and entertainment, government, and news and information media—has exploded. The result is a culture in which many core institutions, including churches, and basic ways of life are continually being radically redefined.

But the coming changes will not be smooth transitions. Although Millennials are leading the way toward the new worldview emphases in America, their rhetoric is often inconsistent with their behavior. This will produce confusion and turbulence.

Our studies of worldview development have shown that people do what they believe. The problem is that people do not always know what they really believe, or sometimes they claim to believe something that they do not. As a result, many people express one belief but live another.

An example of this paradox relates to the well-known Millennial expectation that people should be tolerant of competing ideas. Millennials are aware and protective of their marketplace positioning as the advocates of tolerance. Yet upon measuring their behaviors—such as getting even with people they believe have wronged them, responses to the inequitable or situational treatment of people, or aggressively censoring competing viewpoints or policies—the actions of the generation are indisputably at odds with their alleged embrace of tolerance and diversity.

Consider a couple of examples. Millennials are twice as likely as older adults to specify that the only people they are willing to respect are those who hold the same religious and political views as they do. They also emerged as the generation far more likely than any other to seek revenge against anyone they believe had done them wrong.

Even more significantly, the Millennial generation seems committed to living without God, without the Bible, and without Christian churches as foundations in either their personal life or within American society. In the 1960s and '70s, Baby Boomers opened the floodgates to questioning the validity and need for the nation's existing spiritual foundations. Baby Busters (also known as Gen X) continued that transition, though less emphatically. Millennials are emulating the aggressiveness of the Boomers in their determination to reshape the spiritual contours of the nation, as well as the larger culture itself, according to their preferences and perspectives.

It is hard to imagine a louder, clearer, and more direct challenge to the future of the Christian faith in the United States. If Christian churches, pastors, schools and individuals believe that a biblical Christian faith is important—not just for themselves but also for our nation, the world beyond it and for future generations—time is running out to intelligently and strategically act on that belief before those who so vehemently disagree succeed in destroying the freedoms and opportunities required to preserve the ways of God in this country.

NOTES:

1. Generations in the survey are defined as follows: Millennials (born 1984 to 2002 and aged 18 to 36 at the time of the survey); Generation X or Gen X (born 1965 to 1983); Boomers (born 1946 to 1964); and Builders (born 1927 to 1945).

CHAPTER 9

OUR STRUGGLES WITH ABORTION FLOW FROM WORLDVIEW AMBIGUITY

Public opinion studies during the past quarter century regarding abortion have uncovered several patterns. Among those are the following:

1. Americans know surprisingly little about the processes and laws related to abortion. Despite substantial media attention directed to this lightening-rod issue, most Americans have only a passing knowledge of what abortion entails, what the existing laws permit and prohibit, the distinctive roles of the federal and state governments regarding abortion, and the facts regarding abortion in the marketplace.
2. Abortion is one of the few social issues over which public opinion has remained fluid during the last two decades. While we have seen a solid core of roughly four out of every 10 of adults opposing legalized abortion since the turn of the millennium, and an equal proportion supporting legalized abortion during that time, the remaining 20% or so of the population vacillates between the two poles.
3. As Americans have become less clear about and less beholden to their religious faith, opinions on abortion have been less frequently and less deeply tied to religious

> principles. This is partially explained by most Protestant pastors refusing to teach biblical principles in relation to abortion. It is also a partial result of the nation's general biblical illiteracy, and more specifically its confusion about biblical teaching regarding life. The growing degree of biblical illiteracy, in turn, is related to the public's changing views about the reliability and relevance of the Bible, as well as its increasing belief that the most trustworthy source of moral guidance is personal feelings.

These patterns lead to an important conclusion: If we want to alleviate the widespread anxieties and political conflict related to abortion, we must address the worldview distortions that have brought us to our current standstill. Because worldview dictates our moral choices, the tensions surrounding abortion will remain intense and unresolved until we are able to build worldview consensus around core beliefs and behaviors.

Public Policies and Abortion

Abortion law in the United States has traveled a circuitous path over the last 200 years. The practice was first regulated by state governments in the 1820s and 1830s. Given its current political leanings, you might be surprised to learn that the American Medical Association (AMA) advocated criminalizing abortion in the 1850s. The Catholic Church joined the fray in 1869, calling for a ban on all abortions. A few years later Congress entered the battlefield, banning the distribution of contraceptives and abortion-inducing drugs.

The U.S. Supreme Court became a player in this escalating drama in 1965 by striking down the law prohibiting the distribution of contraceptives to married couples as an indefensible invasion of their privacy. Several years hence the Court restored the right of unmarried couples to have access to contraceptives, again citing their right to privacy. Around the same time, Hawaii and New York became the first states to legalize abortion, with other states soon following their lead.

The most significant abortion case for the U.S. Supreme Court was *Roe v. Wade*, with its decision rendered in January of 1973. In that instance the Court struck down a Texas state law that banned abortion. The effect of doing so was to permit abortions throughout the United States. The court argued that a woman has an implied right to an abortion based on her right to privacy, as detailed in the Fourteenth Amendment to the U.S. Constitution. The court opinion also noted that abortion is not an absolute right. States retain an interest in regulating the practice. The majority opinion then outlined the relative interest of the state based upon the trimester of the pregnancy and the dangers to the health of the mother and fetus.

Its next groundbreaking abortion ruling was *Casey v. Planned Parenthood* in 1992. In that case the justices voted to uphold a woman's right to abort the fetus before "viability," which the court had previously established to be around six months after conception. After hearing the arguments in *Casey*, the Court was primed to rule against abortion rights and to actually strike down *Roe v. Wade* by a 5-4 vote. However, maneuvering behind the scenes by Justices O'Connor and Souter led to a reversal of the vote. They succeeded in persuading Justice Kennedy to change his vote prior to the majority opinion being written and released.

The Court broke new ground again in the 2007 verdict in *Gonzales v. Carhart* by upholding a federal law banning partial-birth abortions. Importantly, the court determined that the ban did not place an undue burden on a woman's right to have an abortion. The majority opinion, written by Justice Kennedy—the same jurist whose changed opinion had flipped the *Casey* verdict 15 years earlier—explained that the ban did not raise any significant obstacles to women having an abortion.

The case argued before the high court in December 2021, *Dobbs v. Jackson Women's Health*, focused upon a Mississippi state law that would effectively ban almost all abortions performed after 15 weeks of pregnancy. Passed by the Mississippi state legislature in 2018, that law was never enacted due to legal challenges resulting in two lower courts vacating the law. The lower court rulings based their determinations on age of viability for the fetus, which had been established as 24 weeks after conception.

The *Dobbs* case stirred considerable emotion and action from both sides of the abortion controversy. People in the "pro-life" camp were hopeful that nearly 50 years of permissive abortion policies would be struck down by the court, putting an end to legalized murder of the pre-born, especially in light of the medical advances since *Roe* that have provided more information about pregnancy and fetal viability. The biggest hope of all, of course, was that *Roe v. Wade* itself would be struck down by the Court.

People in the "pro-choice" camp were hopeful that the high court would rely upon the long-established legal concept of *stare decisis*—the Latin term used to describe reliance upon existing legal precedents. Their optimism was based on the fact that the practice has generally been followed by the high court.

Faith Views and the Choice to be Made

Given that people make their choices about the practical matters of life through the lens of their worldview, what relevant perspectives do most Americans possess to influence their position on abortion? Are they more likely to see abortion as an issue regarding the right to life or as a matter of protecting personal choice? Do Americans view abortion as a spiritual issue or not?

Our most recent surveys on this matter find that Americans are divided in their opinions. Equal numbers of people say they would prefer that *Roe v. Wade* be struck down (38%) as say they want it to be upheld (39%), with nearly one-fourth of adults (23%) not having an opinion. Some of the population segments most supportive of striking down *Roe* are groups expected to be in that camp: SAGE Cons (i.e., Spiritually Active

Governance Engaged Conservative Christians, 76% of whom oppose retaining *Roe* as law), self-identified theological conservatives (61%), Integrated Disciples (i.e., adults with a biblical worldview, 60% of whom oppose *Roe*), and those who attend Pentecostal or charismatic churches (60%).

Interestingly, the research also identified groups that would not necessarily be expected to emerge as strong advocates of eliminating legalized abortion. Those include people who get most of their political news from radio (71%) or from podcasts (77%), people with graduate-level degrees (49%), and individuals from upper-income households (51%). Non-whites are also significantly more likely than whites to favor doing away with the *Roe* ruling (46% versus 34%, respectively).

Although abortion has long been a political "hot potato," only one out of every seven voters in the 2020 election (14%) identified it as one of the top two issues they considered when making their voting decisions. Some voter segments were noteworthy for elevating the importance of abortion in their candidate selection process. Those groups included people who consistently embrace conservative positions on political matters (29% listed abortion as a top-two issue); SAGE Cons (28%); Integrated Disciples (24%); the most church-engaged Christians (22%); people associated with a charismatic or Pentecostal church (20%); and Hispanics (19%).

General Views and America's Future

Data from the *American Worldview Inventory 2021* provides additional insight into the worldview behind people's position on abortion. For instance, a plurality of adults (i.e., the largest share but not a majority) contends that the Bible is ambiguous in its teachings about abortion. They believe that you could make a strong argument both for and against the practice from scriptural teaching. Overall, 41% agreed with that notion, 36% disagreed, and one-quarter of adults (23%) said they did not know.

Similarly, a plurality of adults (48%) said they consider an abortion to be morally acceptable (or not even a moral issue) if the woman has been abandoned by the baby's father and does not feel she can reasonably raise the child on her own. A smaller proportion (43%) said undergoing an abortion for that reason was morally unacceptable, and 9% did not know what to think.

Let's reflect on the spiritual context in which those decisions have been made.

Most adults admit that they do not read the Bible with any regularity, if at all. Why not? Only four out of 10 Americans now deem the Bible to be the true, reliable, and trustworthy words of God. Just 46% believe in the existence of God, as described in the Bible. Barely more than one out of every three believe that absolute moral truths exist. Less than one-third (31%) say that their primary source of moral guidance is the Bible.

Only four out of every 10 adults (39%) believe that life is sacred. And the connection between the purpose and value of our life, and the desires of God is tenuous, at best. Just three out of 10 adults say our purpose is to know, love, and serve God, while twice as many (59%) argue that the purpose of life is to pursue and achieve personal and cultural happiness or satisfaction. A plurality (37%) also believes that life is what we make it; there is no absolute value associated with human life.

Millennials to the Rescue?

Many people assume that the hope of the pro-life movement lies in the hands of the Millennial generation because they are a decidedly pro-life group. Unfortunately, that is not the case. Millennials are not a predominantly pro-life generation.

If you find that a hard pill to swallow, then put together the pieces of the puzzle and come to your own conclusion. Here are the relevant pieces:

- They are the generation *least likely* to believe:
    - Human life is sacred.
    - God is the all-knowing, all-powerful, just and merciful creator of the universe who still rules that universe today.
    - Humankind was created by God.
    - Every person has a God-given purpose in life.
    - People are basically good.
    - To embrace the Golden Rule (i.e., treat others the way you want to be treated).
- They are the generation *most likely* to believe:
    - People are merely biological machines.
    - Human life has no inherent value.
    - The Bible is ambiguous about abortion.

On a more personal level, but germane to a discussion about the perceived value of human life, Millennials are the least likely generation since public opinion polling began to possess an interest in having children.

The impression that Millennials are a pro-life generation may come from the fact that many of the most visible pro-life activists and leaders are young adults. But that is merely another reason why anecdotal evidence cannot be relied upon as a basis for decision-making.

The larger body of objective data indicates that most Millennials are not pushing for America to distance itself from a half-century history of abortions, with our permissive laws leading to more than 62 million unborn children murdered during that period. Attitudinally, Millennials believe in choice more than they believe in absolute moral truth. They would prefer to retain the right to choose between birth or abortion than to trust biblical principles to guide the nation forward.

The Bottom Line Is Worldview

In the end, no matter how we slice the data, people's decisions about the value of life and the permissibility of abortion all come back to worldview.

Consider a very black-and-white examination of those with a biblical worldview and those without one:

- More than nine out of every 10 adults (93%) who have a biblical worldview believe that human life is sacred.
- More than nine out of 10 Integrated Disciples (92%) reject the notion that the Bible is ambiguous about the moral acceptability of abortion.
- Less than one-half of one percent of the Integrated Disciples interviewed said that a woman having an abortion because she was deserted by her partner and felt incapable of raising the child was making a morally acceptable decision.

Worldview Determines Perspectives on Abortion

	Bible is ambiguous in its moral teachings about abortion		Morally acceptable for a woman to have an abortion if abandoned by birth partner and uncomfortable raising the child	
Worldview	Agree	Disagree	Yes	No
Biblical worldview	8%	92%	*%	98%
Marxism	58	27	74	19
Eastern Mysticism	48	29	75	18
Postmodernism	34	24	84	11
Secular Humanism	34	28	81	12
Moralistic Therapeutic Deism	48	27	59	30

* Indicates less than one-half percent. Source: *American Worldview Inventory 2021*, Cultural Research Center at Arizona Christian University; N=2,000 U.S. Adults, 2021.

The idea that "Bible is ambiguous about abortion" is championed by people who lean heavily on other worldviews. More than 70% of people who draw heavily from Marxism, Secular Humanism, Eastern Mysticism, Postmodernism, and even Moralistic Therapeutic Deism believe the Bible can be interpreted multiple ways when it comes to abortion.

Given these perspectives, then, it is not a shock to find that more than three out of every four adults who are adherents of other worldviews support a woman having an abortion if she was deserted by her partner and feels incapable of raising the child. That includes 84% of those who often draw their worldview from Postmodernism; 81% who regularly rely upon Secular Humanism; 75% who draw frequently from Eastern Mysticism; and 74% who lean heavily upon Marxist philosophy.

Addressing the Alleged "Biblical Ambiguity"

It seems apparent that those who claim the Bible can be used to either strongly support or oppose abortion are biblically illiterate. The research certainly supports the notion that pro-abortion individuals are less biblically inclined. They read the Bible less often and are far more likely to dismiss the Bible as myths and stories than to deem it to be God's truth or a reliable source of moral guidance. Perhaps most persuasively, 92% of those who possess the biblical worldview reject the idea of the Bible's ambiguity on this issue, compared to only 20% among those who do not have the biblical worldview. Or, analyzed from a different angle—but producing a similar conclusion—those who reject biblical ambiguity regarding abortion are 13 times more likely to have a biblical worldview than are individuals who champion that idea.

In defense of those who claim the Bible is ambiguous about abortion we could agree that the scriptures do not use the word "abortion," and thus our views on the topic require some deeper study. Further, the verses that are most directly aligned with the issue are not passages that receive much attention from pulpits or are commonly referred to in public discussions about the issue.

However, those who take the time to dig into the Bible to discern God's thoughts on this matter will be confronted with clear statements regarding God's view of and engagement with human life from the moment of conception.

For instance, Jeremiah 1:5 says that God forms us in our mother's womb, a claim further affirmed in Job 31:15. Psalm 139:13-16 not only confirms that God is responsible for creating and forming us in the womb, but that we have been "fearfully and wonderfully made" by Him and that He saw our unformed body even before we were conceived.

The importance of the unborn child is evident in Exodus 21:22-25, which commands anyone who causes the unborn child of a pregnant woman to be harmed in any way to pay in kind. In other words, if the child in the belly of the woman dies, the person who caused that death must also suffer the penalty of death. It is, in effect, the penalty for committing murder, even though the baby is unborn. In God's eyes and law, that unborn child has the same value and rights as a person that lives outside of the womb.

These verses (and others) leave no doubt that human life—both inside and outside of the womb—matters deeply to God. People may seek to determine the value of life based on convenience, feelings, or other indicators, but the One who created human life and rules its every step leaves no doubt as to where He stands on the value of life.

In the end, regardless of what judges, legislators, or media commentators say, the Bible is clear as to God's judgment about abortion. He created humanity, He sustains human life, He provides direction and guidance for our pursuit of a full life, and He takes joy in a life well-lived for His purposes. Our society may choose to disregard His ways but that does not change the fact that His truth principles are absolute, unaltered by our emotions, preferences, arguments, or circumstances.

As the debate continues and most church-going Americans wrestle with their ideas concerning abortion, we might do well to consider the laws and expectations we establish about life in the womb in light of the words of the Apostle Paul: "You say, 'I am allowed to do anything'—but not everything is good for you." (1 Corinthians 6:12, NLT)

CHAPTER 10

CHRISTIANS, THIS IS YOUR WAKE-UP CALL

When I began writing this chapter former President Obama had just finished scolding voters by opining, "We don't have time to be wasting on these phony, trumped up culture wars" but instead, "We should be making it easier for teachers and schools to give our kids the world-class education they deserve."[1]

To put his comments in context, understand that he was criticizing biblically inclined adults for pushing back against cultural leaders in their quest for truth and righteousness. Mr. Obama is shilling for Marxists, Secular Humanists, Postmodernists, and other charlatans to indoctrinate young people—the population whose worldview is being formed for the remainder of their life during those impressionable years—with the lies and immoral choices that characterize those vacuous philosophies of life.

Mr. Obama is just one of thousands of spokespersons for the ways of the world. Competing worldviews are being sold to us by individuals, corporations, and governments. Aberrant thinking and corrupt words are all around us. The forces of darkness are everywhere we go, challenging us in every way imaginable. War has been declared, and those who love God and seek to do His will and live in harmony, and love His principles and commands, are the target.

The Apostle Paul warned us not to be naïve in this battle for our mind and heart. "Don't let anyone capture you with empty philosophies and high-sounding nonsense that come from human thinking and from the spiritual powers of this world, rather than from Christ."[2] Paul understood the nature of the battle we face, cautioning about deception from clever and appealing arguments, conveyed in the most persuasive ways available.[3] Today that means we have to be alert to seduction and manipulation through television, movies, music, video games, books, laws, political speeches, classroom lessons, conversations with peers, and even unbiblical sermons. All of these, and more, are simply the means of promoting the lies of this world.

Every day we live amidst spiritual war—and a significant part of that war is waged on the worldview front. The failure of Christ-followers to consistently live out the biblical worldview in recent decades has given the enemies of God's truth a foothold that has grown into a stronghold. Only God can transform a nation to godliness, but His method continues to be reliance upon imperfect but Christ-loving, Bible-believing people—like you and me—to actively fight for His truth principles and resulting behaviors to prevail.

Consider the breadth of alternative views common across our country these days. If you made a list of the topics addressed by competing worldviews, the list would correspond to the most significant questions of human life: origins of the universe, evolution, truth, moral behavior, life after death, the existence of God, the role of history, the reliability of the Bible, the definition of success, and more. The popular but incorrect views promoted through media, government, schools, and other means then get translated into countless lifestyle applications and infiltrate every decision that each of us makes every day.

Because followers of Christ believe that the Bible contains truth and practical guidance for living, we have a different way of understanding these matters. Our response is often mocked or criticized, sometimes even outlawed, because we usually represent the minority view. Literally 94% of the population does not think biblically with consistency.

The burden is on the shoulders of those with a biblical worldview to explain *why* we believe the Bible is true, *what* we believe the Bible says about any given issue or situation, and to show *how* that truth is applied to life. If we cannot articulate and demonstrate a persuasive perspective on these matters, great numbers of people will suffer the consequences of biblical illiteracy and ungodly living—and our inability to spare them from those consequences. We are not their savior—that's Jesus Christ—but we are the agents of transformation that He uses to bless the world.

Where do we start in a world that has been so thoroughly captivated by rampant deception?

Having spent nearly half a century digging into the recesses of people's minds and hearts through literally hundreds of research studies, and analyzing the responses of hundreds of thousands of Americans, allow me to suggest five arguments that are pervasive and deadly. God will use us to turn the tide in our culture if we remain sensitized to and appalled by these arguments as we encounter them, and if we are prepared and committed to effectively responding.

> **Lie #1:** There is no omniscient, omnipotent, omnipresent God who created us, loves us and wants to know and save us.
>
> **Lie #2:** There is not and cannot be absolute, objective moral truth.
>
> **Lie #3:** The Bible is a book of religious stories that might inspire, entertain or even improve your life sometimes, but it is not the words and principles of a holy deity meant to direct our lives.
>
> **Lie #4:** The purpose of life is not about the desires of an external presence or power. Your life is about you and what gives you pleasure, comfort, and satisfaction.

> **Lie #5:** Human life is neither a precious gift nor of inherent value. Our lives come and go. You, and you alone, determine the nature, value, and trajectory of your life on earth.

Can you discern why these are lies and why they are so powerful?

The more fully and confidently you grasp the biblical truths that destroy such deceptions and are able to clearly and lovingly articulate counter-arguments to the world, the more influence you will have for God's kingdom.

And the research shows that the most powerful way of presenting those arguments is not through your words but through your actions. When you live God's truth for all to see, and have the capacity to explain why you do so, despite the cultural forces aligned against you, you will have incredible power and influence.

What will you do?

Know who you are in Christ and whom you ultimately serve. And enter into His service with the full knowledge that one of the most powerful weapons God gives you is the biblical worldview.

Don't enter the battle unarmed.

NOTES:

1. See "Barack Obama Slapped with Reality Check After He Denounces 'Trumped Up Culture Wars,' 'Fake Outrage,'" Chris Enloe, *The Blaze*, October 24, 2021.
2. Colossians 2:8, NLT
3. Colossians 2:4

APPENDIX 1

BIBLE PASSAGES THAT ENCOURAGE US TO DEVELOP A BIBLICAL WORLDVIEW

(Note: All Scripture is from the *Holy Bible*, New Living Translation, copyright 1988, 2004. Used by permission of Tyndale House Publishers Inc., Wheaton, IL. All rights reserved.)

Romans 12:2

Don't copy the behavior and customs of this world, but let God transform you into the new person by changing the way you think. Then you will learn to know God's will for you, which is good and pleasing and perfect.

Colossians 2:8

Don't let anyone capture you with empty philosophies and high-sounding nonsense that come from human thinking and from the spiritual powers of this world, rather than from Christ.

2 Corinthians 10:3-5

We are human, but we don't wage war as humans do. We use God's mighty weapons, not worldly weapons, to knock down the strongholds of human reasoning and to destroy false arguments. We destroy every proud obstacle that keeps people from knowing God. We capture their rebellious thoughts and teach them to obey Christ.

Ecclesiastes 12:13-14

That's the whole story. Here now is my final conclusion: Fear God and obey his commands, for this is everyone's duty. God will judge us for everything we do, including every secret thing, whether good or bad.

Isaiah 55:8

"My thoughts are nothing like your thoughts," says the LORD. "And my ways are far beyond anything you could imagine."

Proverbs 2:2-8

Tune your ears to wisdom and concentrate on understanding. Cry out for insight, and ask for understanding. Search for them as you would for silver; seek them like hidden treasures. Then you will understand what it means to fear the Lord, and you will gain knowledge of God. For the Lord grants wisdom! From his mouth come knowledge and understanding. He grants a treasure of common sense to the honest. He is a shield to those who walk with integrity. He guards the paths of the just and protects those who are faithful to him.

Proverbs 3:5-7

Trust in the Lord with all your heart; do not depend on your own understanding. Seek his will in all you do, and he will show you which path to take. Don't be impressed with your own wisdom. Instead, fear the Lord and turn away from evil.

Colossians 3:17

And whatever you do or say, do it as a representative of the Lord Jesus, giving thanks through him to God the Father.

Proverbs 1:7

Fear of the Lord is the foundation of true knowledge, but fools despise wisdom and discipline.

John 17:17

Make them holy by your truth; teach them your word, which is truth.

Deuteronomy 6:2-9

You and your children and grandchildren must fear the Lord your God as long as you live. If you obey all his decrees and commands, you will enjoy a long life. Listen closely, Israel, and be careful to obey. Then all will go well with you, and you will have many children in the land flowing with milk and honey, just as the Lord, the God of your ancestors, promised you. "Listen, O Israel! The Lord is our God, the Lord alone. And you must love the Lord your God with all your heart, all your soul, and all your strength. And you must commit yourselves wholeheartedly to these commands that I am giving you today. Repeat them again and again to your children. Talk about them when you are at home and when you are on the road, when you are going to bed and when you are getting up. Tie them to your hands and wear them on your forehead as reminders. Write them on the doorposts of your house and on your gates."

1 John 2:15-17

Do not love this world nor the things it offers you, for when you love the world, you do not have the love of the Father in you. For the world offers only a craving for physical pleasure, a craving for everything we see, and pride in our achievements and possessions. These are not from the Father, but are from this world. And this world is fading away, along with everything that people crave. But anyone who does what pleases God will live forever.

Hebrews 4:12

For the word of God is alive and powerful. It is sharper than the sharpest two-edged sword, cutting between soul and spirit, between joint and marrow. It exposes our innermost thoughts and desires.

Colossians 2:20-23

You have died with Christ, and he has set you free from the spiritual powers of this world. So why do you keep on following the rules of the world, such as, "Don't handle! Don't taste! Don't touch!"? Such rules are mere human teachings about things that deteriorate as we use them. These rules may seem wise because they require strong devotion, pious self-denial, and severe bodily discipline. But they provide no help in conquering a person's evil desires.

2 Timothy 4:3-4

For a time is coming when people will no longer listen to sound and wholesome teaching. They will follow their own desires and will look for teachers who will tell them whether their itching ears want to hear. They will reject the truth and chase after myths.

Romans 8:5-8

Those who are dominated by the sinful nature think about sinful things, but those who are controlled by the Holy Spirit think about things that please the Spirit. So letting your sinful nature control your mind leads to death. But letting the Spirit control your mind leads to life and peace. For the sinful nature is always hostile to God. It never did obey God's laws, and it never will. That's why those who are still under the control of their sinful nature can never please God.

Matthew 15:18-20

The words you speak come from the heart – that's what defiles you. For from the heart come evil thoughts, murder, adultery, all sexual immorality, theft, lying, and slander. These are what defile you. Eating with unwashed hands will never defile you.

2 Cor 5:15-17

He died for everyone so that those who receive his new life will no longer live for themselves. Instead, they will live for Christ, who died and was raised for them. So we have stopped evaluating others from a human point of view. At one time we thought of Christ merely from a human point of view. How differently we know him now! This means that anyone who belongs to Christ has become a new person. The old life is gone; a new life has begun!

Galatians 6:14-15

As for me, may I never boast about anything except the cross of our Lord Jesus Christ. Because of that cross, my interest in this world has been crucified, and the world's interest in me has also died. It doesn't matter whether we have been circumcised or not. What counts is whether we have been transformed into a new creation.

John 8:31-32

Jesus said to the people who believed in him, "You are truly my disciples if you remain faithful to my teachings. And you will know the truth, and the truth will set you free."

Acts 17:2, 11, 17, 30

As was Paul's custom, he went to the synagogue service, and for three Sabbaths in a row he used the Scriptures to reason with the people… And the people of Berea were more open-minded than those in Thessalonica, and they listened eagerly to Paul's message. They searched the Scriptures day after day to see if Paul and Silas were teaching the truth... He went to the synagogue to reason with the Jews and the God-fearing Gentiles, and he spoke daily in the public square to all who happened to be there…

God overlooked people's ignorance about these things in earlier times, but now he commands everyone everywhere to repent of their sins and turn to him.

James 1:22-25

But don't just listen to God's word. You must do what it says. Otherwise, you are only fooling yourselves. For if you listen to the word and don't obey, it is like glancing at your face in a mirror. You see yourself, walk away, and forget what you look like. But if you look carefully into the perfect law that sets you free, and if you do what it says and don't forget what you heard, then God will bless you for doing it.

APPENDIX 2

ABOUT THE AUTHOR

George Barna is a professor at Arizona Christian University (ACU) and co-founded the Cultural Research Center based at the University. His focus at ACU is worldview assessment and development, and cultural transformation. He was the founder and leader of The Barna Group (which he sold in 2009) and the American Culture and Faith Institute (2011-2018). He has been the President of Metaformation, a research and communications company, since 2009. Barna serves as the Senior Research Fellow for the Center for Biblical Worldview at the Family Research Council. He is also a Townsend Fellow, associated with Concordia University.

Barna has conducted groundbreaking research on worldview, cultural transformation, ministry applications, spiritual development, and election strategy. He has provided research strategy to several hundred parachurch ministries, thousands of Christian churches, the U.S. military, and numerous non-profit and for-profit organizations, and has provided polling and strategy input for four presidential candidates.

Barna has written or co-authored more than 50 books, mostly addressing cultural and religious trends, leadership, spiritual development, church dynamics, and cultural transformation. They include *New York Times* bestsellers and several award-winning books. His books have been translated into more than a dozen languages.

He lists his most influential books as *The Frog in the Kettle*, *Transforming Children into Spiritual Champions, Revolution, Think Like Jesus, Pagan Christianity*, and *Maximum Faith*. His most recent books are part of the *American Worldview Inventory* series.

Before his current role at Arizona Christian University, he taught at several universities (Pepperdine University, Azusa Pacific University, Biola University, and Dallas Baptist University) and seminaries (including Reformed Theological Seminary, Talbot, and others). He has been the teaching pastor of a large, multi-ethnic church, pastor of a house church, and an elder at three churches. An in-demand public speaker, Barna has spoken at hundreds of public events during his career. He is also a frequent guest on numerous platforms, discussing his research findings and their implications.

After graduating summa cum laude from Boston College with a degree in Sociology, Barna earned two master's degrees from Rutgers University and received a doctorate from Dallas Baptist University. Born in New York City, he married his wife, Nancy, in 1978. They have three daughters and three grandchildren. They live on the central California coast and in the Phoenix area.

APPENDIX 3

ABOUT THE CULTURAL RESEARCH CENTER AND ARIZONA CHRISTIAN UNIVERSITY

The Cultural Research Center (CRC) at Arizona Christian University was founded in August 2019 to conduct cutting-edge cultural and biblical worldview studies to provide credible research and resources to inform and mobilize strategic engagement in cultural transformation. The starting point of transforming culture is to get a clear picture of the worldviews that animate its landscape.

The goal of the Cultural Research Center is to become the nation's premiere biblical worldview measurement hub. Arizona Christian University will continue to provide worldview education to college students, but that activity is just one of the many that relate to the core mission of ACU—expanding the biblical worldview in America—both in the Church and in American culture.

As the biblical worldview research and resource arm of Arizona Christian University, the Cultural Research Center provides research and resources to individuals, families, churches, schools and universities, and organizations that seek to strategically increase the level of biblical worldview among people of faith and within American culture.

The Cultural Research Center also collaborates with other leading national organizations, with the goal of providing reliable research and effective resources for biblical worldview understanding within all areas of American culture.

The Cultural Research Center serves Arizona Christian University's worldview development efforts by measuring student worldview development using the *ACU Student Worldview Inventory* (administered throughout each student's academic career). ACU is committed to biblical worldview development and assessment in all facets of the student experience.

The Cultural Research Center at Arizona Christian University is located on the school's campus in Glendale, Arizona, in the Phoenix metropolitan area. Access to the results from past surveys conducted by the CRC, as well as additional information about the Cultural Research Center, are available at www.CulturalResearchCenter.com.

The Cultural Research Center team includes:

George Barna, CRC Director of Research. Barna is the nation's leading researcher in the area of faith and culture. He co-founded the CRC as its Director of Research and is a professor at Arizona Christian University. He is also the founder of the Barna Group, a research company that has set the standard for understanding trends in American culture. Barna has written more than 50 books, including numerous award winners and *New York Times* bestsellers. His full bio is available in Appendix 2.

Tracy F. Munsil, Ph.D., CRC Executive Director. Dr. Munsil is an Associate Professor of Political Science at Arizona Christian University. She created the University's political science program and chaired the ACU Department of Government, History and Philosophy for eight years prior to becoming CRC Executive Director. Dr. Munsil also chaired the collaborative process to develop the ACU CORE, which integrates biblical worldview into the University's distinctive liberal arts curriculum. She developed a passion for biblical worldview while home-educating her eight children for 14 years. Her Doctorate in Political Science in 2011 was her third degree from Arizona State University, after earning both a Political Science Master's and a Bachelor's of Science in Journalism. In addition to her work as CRC's Executive Director, Dr. Munsil also serves as Editor of Arizona Christian University Press. She was appointed by the Governor of Arizona and confirmed by the Arizona Senate for two terms on the Arizona Commission on Appellate Court Appointments.

Monica Lievsay, CRC Research Fellow. Monica Lievsay served as the Research Fellow of the Cultural Research Center from October 2021 through March 2022. She is also an alumnus of Arizona Christian University. She graduated with a masters in Comparative Social Change from both University College Dublin and Trinity University in Ireland. She brought research expertise in the areas of psychology, theology, and education, and has completed work in the area of the development of procrastination in children.

Annabelle Camoirano, ACU Communication Major, Arizona Christian University Press Intern Fall 2021. Annabelle helped in manuscript proofreading and book design for *The American Worldview Inventory 2021-22* as part of her Fall 2021 internship with Arizona Christian University Press.

Caelan Merryman, ACU Political Science Major, Cultural Research Center Intern Spring 2022. Caelan assisted in various capacities during his Spring 2022 internship.

ABOUT ARIZONA CHRISTIAN UNIVERSITY

Arizona Christian University (ACU) is one of the fastest-growing Christian universities in America and ranked by *U.S. News & World Report* as the No. 1 Undergraduate Teaching Institution in the West. Arizona Christian University provides a biblically integrated, liberal arts education equipping graduates to serve the Lord Jesus Christ in all aspects of life as leaders of influence and excellence. Arizona Christian University exists to educate and equip followers of Christ to transform culture with the truth.

Arizona Christian University is an accredited, private, non-profit, Christian university in the Phoenix metropolitan area. ACU is an award-winning, culturally and theologically conservative university where students and their professors are serious about deepening their Christian faith and where relationships and community deeply matter. It offers a wide variety of degrees preparing students for successful careers, while remaining committed to its vision of transforming culture with biblical truth.

Students actively engage in biblically integrated academics and gain a liberal arts foundation with critical thinking skills that last a lifetime. Spiritual development is integrated within the University experience, where all four-year campus students receive a minor in Biblical Studies, attend chapel twice a week, and complete spiritual formation and service hours each semester.

Arizona Christian University is the nation's premiere worldview university. One of its key distinctives is its emphasis on biblical worldview integration through the University's CORE Christian Liberal Arts curriculum, as well as in their chosen academic discipline. The ACU Student Worldview Inventory measures the worldview development from freshmen year through graduation. Further information about Arizona Christian University is accessible at www.arizonachristian.edu.

APPENDIX 4

ABOUT THE AMERICAN WORLDVIEW INVENTORY 2021-2022

The *American Worldview Inventory 2021 (AWVI)* is the second wave of an annual series of surveys that estimates how many adults have a biblical worldview. The *AWVI* survey was developed in cooperation with the faculty and administration of Arizona Christian University. The resulting survey went through several rounds of development and pre-testing before being rolled out nationally.

The assessment is based on 51 worldview-related questions drawn from eight categories of worldview application, measuring both beliefs and behavior. These categories are:

1. Bible, Truth, and Morals
2. Faith Practices
3. Family and the Value of Life
4. God, Creation, and History
5. Human Character and Nature
6. Lifestyle, Behavior, and Relationships
7. Purpose and Calling
8. Sin, Salvation, and God Relationship

In addition to the worldview questions, the survey also contains an array of demographic and theolographic (i.e., religious background) questions. In total, the *AWVI* instrument incorporates 68 questions and takes respondents an average of 16 minutes to complete.

The *AWVI 2021* focused on seven competing worldviews held by American adults, measuring both belief and behavior consistent with those worldviews. Those seven worldviews are:

1. Biblical Theism
2. Secular Humanism
3. Moralistic Therapeutic Deism
4. Postmodernism
5. Nihilism
6. Eastern Mysticism
7. Marxism

AWVI 2021 was undertaken in February 2021 among a nationally representative sample of 2,000 adults. The data set includes responses from 1,000 interviews completed with a nationwide random sample of adults via telephone, plus another 1,000 adults who completed interviews conducted online through use of a national panel of adults.

A survey of 2,000 randomly sampled individuals has an estimated maximum sampling error of approximately plus or minus 2 percentage points, based on the 95% confidence interval. Additional levels of indeterminable error may occur in surveys based upon non-sampling activity. The level of estimated sampling error is larger for subsets of the aggregate sample.

This publication, *American Worldview Inventory 2021-22*, provides a summary and detailed analysis of the worldview findings from the research conducted using the *American Worldview Inventory 2021*.

CPSIA information can be obtained
at www.ICGtesting.com
Printed in the USA
LVHW080531021022
729732LV00003B/11